We, the Northern Cheyenne People: Our Land, Our History, Our Culture

WE,
THE NORTHERN
CHEYENNE PEOPLE

Our Land, Our History, Our Culture

CHIEF DULL KNIFE COLLEGE, LAME DEER, MONTANA

Chief Dull Knife College
P O Box 98
Lame Deer, MT 59043
406 477 6215

Library of Congress
Cataloging-in-Publication Data

Project management
Suzanne G Fox
Red Bird Publishing, Inc , Bozeman, MT
Graphic design
Carol Beehler, Bethesda, MD
Printed by Artcraft Printers, Billings MT

The paper used in this publication meets the
minimum requirements of American National
Standard for Information Sciences—Permanence
of Paper for Printed Library Materials, ANSI 739 48-
1984

Front cover *Voohebeva*, the Morning Star rises
near dawn outside a Native American Church
gathering The morning star is the symbol for the
Northern Cheyenne people It is greeted as an
ancient old man each morning by the Keepers of
the Sacred Covenants Photograph by John
Warner

Back cover The Chief Dull Knife College campus
is located in Lame Deer, MT Photograph by
Kathleen Beartusk

Nesaa'evatonéšenéheše vo'éstanéhevéheme-
tsemehaeheševo'éstanehevetse
Tsemona'e vo'éstanehevestótse neto'séhene'enanone
Netaveestanonéstse móxe'éstonemáheonótse, nonohpa
Neka'éškonéhamaneo'o tseohketséhe'óhtseo'o
Naa tsetáhene'enanove he'tohe tsemona'e vo'éstanehevestótse

We can no longer live the way we used to
There is a new way of life that we are going to know
Let us ask for schools, that way
our children can attend them
and learn this new way of life

—CHIEF DULL KNIFE (Vooheheva)

Contents

Preface and Acknowledgments

Dr. Richard Little Bear

CHIEF DULL KNIFE COLLEGE was able to produce *We, The Northern Cheyenne People Our Land, Our History, Our Culture* with a grant from the Montana State Legislature and Governor Brian Schweitzer. The funding for the Tribal Histories and Equipment project is gratefully acknowledged.

This project has been an interesting one for all of the people who worked on it. It was a good learning, reading, writing, and researching experience. There were, however, some challenges along the way. One challenge was accessibility of research materials. While the researchers did find much new material, there are still so many sources, so many collections, so many museums that need to be visited to get information, especially the information that was provided by people who were close to the pre-reservation culture. Time constraints and always increasing costs limited the accessibility of these sources.

Another challenge was the plethora of books that have already been written about both the Northern and Southern Cheyenne people starting with George Bird Grinnell's accounts. More recently is the book *A History of the Cheyenne People* written by Tom Weist and published by the Montana Council for Indian Education from Billings, MT, under the leadership of Dr. Hap Gilliland. This book extensively used the elders of the day, some of whom were only one generation removed from the time of the buffalo-centered culture. Chief Dull Knife College uses this as a text book for its Cheyenne history class. Weist's book posed a challenge because it had amply covered the history of the Cheyenne people from earliest times up to the mid-1970s.

It became clear that some subject areas of that book needed strengthening and those are the areas that this present effort attempts to address. People who use *We, the Northern Cheyenne People Our Land, Our History, Our Culture* need to use the Weist book in tandem. Our book tries to strengthen those subject areas that were not adequately covered in the Weist book, including women, spirituality, energy issues, educational issues, and veterans of the armed forces. Not including the topic of women was a major oversight in many of the history books. There were cursory accounts of North Woman, The Girl Who Saved Her Brother, Bessie Harris (the first female Northern Cheyenne council woman), and Geri Small (the first female Northern Cheyenne tribal president). The list of potential subjects is almost endless. Even this book has not done justice to the place that women have earned in Northern Cheyenne culture and history.

In each subject, the writers tried to be as comprehensive as possible and to include all who were involved, but inevitably there are mistakes. For anybody who is offended by being excluded or by having a member of their families excluded, it was purely unintentional. The writers were meticulous in providing footnotes for citations so the right person received recognition for their efforts and to make the work of subsequent researchers easier.

Another challenge was finding Northern Cheyenne writers and researchers, some of whom also had the added skill of being able to talk and understand the Cheyenne language. People with this mix of skills were difficult to find, but we found several. Some of the writers and photographers had full-time jobs elsewhere, but they managed to fulfill their assignment on a timely basis. Another challenge was the deadline, which, even though it was extended from June 30 to Dec. 31, 2007, was still not enough time. Some parts of the history were slighted, but everybody did the best they could.

But so much for the challenges. There is so much information in various museums, collections, universities, colleges, and the internet that could be mined forever. This book has been a modest effort when compared with the information that is still available and is ripe for another or a continuing history project.

By using the Tom Weist book as a "reverse template," this project attempted to fill in the gaps of that book. This is no easy task since the panorama of Cheyenne history, both Northern and Southern, is immense, tragic, unendingly interesting, and eventually uplifting. This is a story filled with many losses: of land, of loved ones, of spirituality, of language, of culture, of education, but even with these losses there have always been replacements for those aspects of the Northern Cheyenne culture that slipped away. Some of them may not have been the best replacements like alcohol, drugs, and poverty, but the Northern Cheyenne are learning to cope with their deleterious effects. Once the Cheyennes realize that alcohol and drugs are the new enemy, even more deadly than a hundred Custers and Chivingtons, their ability to cope with the present situations will become easier to address.

For instance, the Cheyenne people lost a lot of land, but through huge sacrifices of all Cheyennes, a treasured piece was retained in southeastern Montana. Some Crow Indians say that if it weren't for them, the Northern Cheyenne would not have a reservation This assertion is a convenient fiction which does a complete disservice to the many Cheyennes who died on the northward journey home in the late 1800s

Of loved ones, we have gained more relatives because the population of the Northern Cheyenne people is probably the most it has ever been Of spirituality, for good or bad, the people have acquired additional ways of expressing our spirituality through organized, European-based non-Cheyenne religions, all the while retaining the Native American Church, the Sun Dance, the fasting ceremony, the sweat lodge, and the reverence for sites sacred to Cheyenne since time immemorial

Of the Cheyenne language much has been lost but there is still a group of older people who have dedicated themselves to preserving the language, not as an artifact for linguists and anthropologists to dissect, but as a contemporary, viable, and influential presence Again, for good or bad, another language, English has become an integral, everyday part of Cheyenne lives Actually, mastering both languages has opened doors of opportunity for bilingual and monolingual Cheyennes alike Of culture, it has necessarily changed from the previous, buffalo- and horse-centered culture of the late 1800s to a computer-, iPod-, text-message-, television-driven culture

Yet the Cheyennes still retain our honoring ceremonies our give-way ceremonies dances songs, and ways of worship and interaction with each other We still enjoy just getting together, preferably with the prospect of a good traditional meal Of education slowly Cheyenne people are beginning to embrace the white man's education and its systems The Cheyenne people are slowly recovering from the highly punitive version of this education that was introduced to Cheyenne people when the reservation-era began Now there are Cheyennes with bachelor, master and doctoral degrees in law, pharmacy, education, dentistry and more educated people are in the future This latter development can only bode well for the whole Cheyenne tribe

This book strove for realism so as not to perpetuate the romanticized notion of Northern Cheyenne people For example, while the Cheyenne value system emphasizes being the original environmentalists and being good caretakers of the land, there is a lot of trash on the reservation The book also strove to include material that had not been included in other history books The writers were not always successful trying to do this There was just too much material Included were those aspects of Cheyenne culture which are unchangeable, like the trek north from Oklahoma

What were omitted were accounts about the little people (*voestanehesono*), the two-faced people (*hestovatohkeo'o*) water monsters (*mehneo'o*), ghosts (*seohto*), Cheyenne humor (*nevoetohta'hanestotse*), and the contemporary (winter 2007)

turmoil being experienced by all of the Northern Cheyenne people The list could go on and on Readers who look for accounts of the above items will just have to do their own research, which is not a bad idea Reading Cheyenne history is an exhilarating journey

Cheyenne Creation Stories

INTRODUCTION

L EGENDS COMPRISE WHAT is probably the oldest surviving form of oral literature known to man Each group of people has had its own explanation
for the creation of the earth and man, each has had its own way of account-
ing for its history Handed down from generation to generation, some of the more
important legends of the Cheyenne are still told today

The legends in this collection appear to be among the oldest told by the
Northern Cheyenne In importance, they rank second only to the legends about
Sweet Medicine, the Cheyenne culture hero and prophet

How THE EARTH *(Ho'e)* WAS MADE

Long, long ago, before there were people, water was everywhere *Ma'heo'o*, the
Creator, was floating on the water All of the water birds were swimming nearby—
the ducks, geese, swans, and other birds that swim Ma'heo'o called to them and
asked them to bring him some earth

One after another, the birds dove down through the deep water, searching for
earth The large birds tried again and again, but they couldn't reach the bottom
At last a small blue duck (a coot or mud-hen) came to the surface with a dab of
mud in its bill

The duck swam to Ma'heo'o, who took the mud and worked it between his
fingers until it dried and turned to dust He took the dust and placed it in little
pieces atop the water Each pile of dust became land that grew and grew until, as
far as the eye could see, there was land everywhere That is how the earth we walk
on was made

The Thunder and the Winter Man

After Ma'heo'o made the earth, He took from his right side a rib and, and from it made a man. He took a rib from the man's left side and, from it, made a woman. He put the woman far to the north and the man far to the south.

Then Ma'heo'o stood between them with his back to the rising sun and spoke to them. "In that direction," he said and here he pointed to the south, 'you will find many kinds of birds and animals that are different from those found in this direction," and here he pointed to the north, where the woman stood. "The birds that live in the south will go to the north in the summer. Where the woman lives, it will be cold, and the grass and trees will not grow well. There will be few of them. But, where the man is, everything will grow: trees, bushes, and grass."

In the north lives Ho im' a ho, *(Hoema'haahe)* the Winter Man. He obeys the woman in the north and takes pity on no one for he is power that brings snow and cold, sickness, and death.

The Thunder (or Thunderbird) *(Nonoma'e)* lives in the south. He is controlled by the man in the south and is the power that brings fire, warmth, and life.

Twice each year the Thunder and the Winter Man come together in conflict. At the end of summer, when the streams are low and the grass has been burnt by the sun, the Winter Man comes down from the north. "Move back to the place from which you came!" he tells the Thunder. "I want to spread about the earth, freezing things and covering everything with snow." Then the Thunder moves back to the south.

Toward spring, when the days are growing longer, the Thunder returns from the south. "Go back!" he tells the Winter Man. "Return to the place from which you came! I want to warm the earth, to turn things green and make the grass grow." Then the Winter Man moves back to the north and the Thunder comes forward, bringing rain and making things grow again.

The Great Race

After making the earth, Ma'heo'o took some dirt (or mud) and formed it in the shape of a human being. He blew breath into the mouth and the person came alive.

After a time, there were more people, and Ma'heo'o taught them how to live, using Indian turnips and wild fruits, small animals, and other foods which they could eat. Then he taught them how to make and use spears so they could hunt game.

It is said that, for a time, the people and the animals lived as friends yet, later, the buffalo began to eat people. This was before the So'taaeo'o (Suhtaio) and the Tsetsehestahese (Tsistsistas) joined in one tribe [1]

In that time, there lived a young So'taetane (Suhtai) man who had a strange dream In his dream, he shot an arrow at a buffalo, but it turned and hit another, standing far away, in the side

When he awoke the young man soon forgot about his dream But that night it came to him again Then, on the third night, the dream came to him once more Now he began to worry about it Finally, he told the old men about his dream and asked them what it meant They told him not to worry, that it probably didn't mean anything

On the fourth night, the dream came to him again When he awoke, he decided to find out just what the dream meant Before the sun rose, he got his bow and arrows and started out

Soon he came upon some buffalo so he hid in the brush by a creek where they were coming down to water When they came closer, he shot an arrow at one, but the arrow turned and hit another buffalo, a young cow that was standing some distance away Now the young man knew that his dream had come true

The buffalo cow wasn't badly hurt She turned around several times with the arrow hanging from her side, and then she started walking The boy followed her Reaching the top of the ridge, he saw that she was walking slowly and was not far ahead, so he cut behind the hills, hoping to cut her off

When he saw her again, she was even further away This puzzled the boy He decided to follow her and stayed on her trail until sundown Finally he decided to return to camp He would look for the buffalo the next morning for, by then, she might be lying down, dead or seriously wounded

The next morning he picked up her trail and followed it across a long flat Ahead, he saw a lone tipi As he neared the tipi, a little boy ran outside and came to meet him, calling him 'father "

' Mother is ready," the little boy told him "She has prepared a meal for you, and you are to come in and eat "

The young man took the little boy's hand, and the boy led him into the tipi Inside, there was a young woman She greeted him as though she were his wife and the little boy their son The tipi was furnished with a bed, willow backrests, and clay cooking pots The woman gave him a meal of turnips and dry fruit Later, they went to bed like a family, planning to move the camp the next morning

When he awoke the young man found himself looking up at the sky The tipi was gone So were the woman and the little boy The young man quickly got up and began searching the ground for tracks

He soon found their tracks and began following them These led in the same direction that he had followed the day before He followed their trail all morning until, in the distance, he saw the tipi

As he approached, the little boy ran out to greet him once more Everything happened just as it had the night before. They ate a meal and later went to bed. The next morning, when the young man awoke, the tipi was gone.

This happened a third time and fourth, just as it happened twice before. On the fourth morning, while the young man was following the tracks of the woman and the little boy, he came to a high ridge. Below, he saw a buffalo herd that stretched as far as the eye could see. He followed the tracks down the ridge toward the herd and crossed a dry sandy place. Here the tracks disappeared and became the tracks of a buffalo cow with a small calf alongside.

As he neared the heard, a small yellow calf ran towards him. 'Father,' said the calf, "they are going to try and kill you! They will line many of the calves in a row, and you will have to guess which one I am. Watch for a calf that shakes his right ear, then pass on by turn, and point at him. That will be me. If you guess right, they won't be able to hurt you."

Everything happened just as the calf had told him. The calves lined up. Then the young man heard a great voice, the voice of one of the buffalo bulls, saying, "Come, find your son!"

The young man went down the line of calves. He watched until he saw one of them shake his right ear. Then he turned pointed, and said, "That is my son!"

Three more times they tested him. And each time the calf came to him and told him to watch for his signal. The buffalo calf shook his tail, then he winked his eye, and next he raised a hind foot. Each time, the young man saw him and said, "That is my son." The buffalo could not harm him.

Finally the herd moved on and across the river. The young man followed, but before he crossed, the calf came to him once more and gave him a dry root to hold, to keep him from sinking into the water.

In the days that followed, the young man was put through many tests each one he passed with the help of his son, the buffalo calf.

One day the yellow calf came to him and said, "My grandfather still wishes to kill you. Now you must race him along a narrow ledge. You will first have to choose between two sticks, a red painted stick and a black one. Take the one on the outside, the black one. That means you will have to race on the outside, by the cliff. That way he wont be able to crush you against the bank. But be careful! Watch his horns! When he turns to come at you, drop to the ground. He'll miss you and go over the cliff."

And so the young man chose the black stick, the one on the outside. He lined up beside the grandfather buffalo. Then they began to run! By the time they reached the halfway point, they were still running side by side. Suddenly the buffalo turned on him! The young man was ready and quickly dropped to the ground! The buffalo missed him, but then he couldn't stop he went over the cliff and was killed.

After the grandfather buffalo was killed, the other buffalo came together in a great gathering. Now in those days all animals had the power to appear as human beings; when the young man came close, he saw that the buffalo had all turned into human beings. Some old men were sitting together in a row, and they called to him and greeted him by putting their arms around his neck or shoulders in the old Indian way.

Then the buffalo men met in council. They decided that there should be one final great race. If the young man won, the people would eat the buffalo. Never again would the buffalo eat the people. But, if the young man lost, he was to be killed and eaten![1]

Now all the birds and animals came together and began to get ready for the great race. They painted themselves. The bald eagle rubbed white clay over his head and neck, made a spot back on his side, and painted the rest of his body brown. The antelope painted himself yellow with white markings.

The buffalo chose a cow named Slim Walking Woman to run for them. She was fast and has never been beaten. She painted herself brown all over.

All of the animals except the magpie and the bear chose to be on the side of the buffalo. The magpie chose to race on the side on the young man.[2]

The bear said, "I won't be on either side. I'll eat anything!" The bear could eat plants as well as meat.

Just as the great race was about to begin, the animals crowded around Slim Walking Woman. Coyote said, 'If the man wins, I won't live the way I do now. I'll live up on the hill, and I'll sing this song." Then he howled just like coyotes do today.

The bald eagle made a whistling noise and said, "If the man wins, I'll sing this song, and my home will be in the air between the earth and the sky."

Then a little brown bird said, "If the man wins, I'll play with the children. They can chase me in the rosebushes."

Now they were ready to start the race. A coyote and a big wolf howled, and the race began, towards the east!

The magpie began to soar, higher and higher into the sky; soon she was far behind the others. The young man ran as fast as he could, keeping pace with the faster animals. Then some of the animals began to tire and fall behind. Yet the buffalo cow kept on running as fast as she could. After a time she, too, began to grow tired, and the buffalo called to her, urging her on. And all this time the magpie was far behind the others, soaring higher and higher.

Some of the animals ran with such fury that they began bleeding at the mouth, turning the ground red. Then, one by one, they began falling by the wayside.

When the bear came to the first animal that had fallen, he stopped and ate him.

Now the race was almost over Suddenly the magpie began to swoop down through the air so fast that she soared across the finish line first, winning the race for the people!

The old buffalo bull called the young man over "You have won," they told him "From now on, you shall be above all the animals We will supply you with our meat skins, and bones And we will teach you how to give a Sun Dance "

Soon the animals began to scatter and go their own way They had decided that none of them was to look back But, as they were leaving, the coyote looked back Even today, whenever a coyote slinks off, he still looks back over his shoulder Each of the animals kept the colors which they still wear

Ever since then, man has had the right to use animal flesh After the race, whenever the people hunted the buffalo, they ran away for having lost the great race, they were afraid of everything

In the old days, the Cheyennes never ate the sweetbreads (thymus gland) found in the throat of the buffalo This was considered to be human fat that had lodged there during the time when the buffalo ate the people Also, they never killed a magpie for its flesh They remembered the great race and how the magpie had won it for the people

Today you can still see the place where the great race was run It is in the Black Hills, near a place called the Buffalo Gap There, a path runs right around the hills The Cheyenne still call this place the Race Track

West of Bear Butte, the Sacred Mountain, near the town of Sundance, WY, the buffalo priests held their Sun Dance Since then, this sacred ceremony has belonged to the So'taa'e (Suhtai), who call themselves the Buffalo People

Today, whenever a Sun Dance is put up, people remember the great race and thank Ma'heo'o for the way it turned out

OLD WOMANS WATER[3] MAIAMAAHE HEHO'HAME'E

Long ago the people camped near a knoll where a spring came out of the rock This spring is known as Old Woman's The opening of the camp faced toward the spring

In the morning, the people began playing the hoop game [4] Soon a young man came from the right side of the camp and stood watching them He wore only a breechcloth and was painted yellow all over and striped down with the fingers On his chest was painted a small red circle while on his back, there was a red half moon There were red stripes around his wrists and ankles His face was painted black beneath his eyes He had a yellow down feather on his scalplock and wore his robe with the hair side out

After a time, another young man came from the left side of the camp and stood watching the hoop game. His paint and dress were identical to that worn by the first young man. Both were surprised when they saw the other.

"My friends," the first young man said to the people, "stop your game for a moment." He asked the other young man to come toward him, and they met in the center of the camp.

"Why do you mock me?" asked the young man. "That is what I want to know," said the other young man. "I think you are making fun of me, painting and dressing just as I do."

"Who gave you your paint, where did you get it?" asked the first young man. "Who gave you yours?" asked the other. The young man pointed to the spring. "My paint came from there." he said.

"My paint came from there also," said the other. "Let us help these people," the first young man said finally. The other agreed with this.

"Warriors," said the young man, "each of you will feel happy this day." All of the people heard this. Then the other young man said this, too.

The two young men turned and walked over to the spring while the people watched. The first young man covered his head with his robe and plunged beneath the water, through the opening from which it came. Then the other followed.

They came up inside the knoll and saw an old woman sitting there inside the lodge. "Come in, my grandchild." she said to each of them. She took them in her arms and held them, and then she had them sit on either side of her.

"Why didn't you come sooner?" she asked. "Why have you gone hungry for so long? Now that you have come, I must do something for your people."

Nearby were two clay jars. She set them before her and then brought out two plates, one was filled with buffalo meat and the other was filled with corn.

'Come, my children, eat the meat,' she told them. The meat was very good, and they ate quickly yet the plate remained full. The same thing happened when they ate the corn. When they finally finished eating, both of the dishes were still full.

Then the old woman untied the feathers they wore and threw them into the fire. She painted each of them with red paint, striped them, and then repainted their wrists and ankles, the sun and the half moon yellow. Finally she reached out over the fire and brought out two down feathers painted red and tied them to their scalplocks.

"Look that way." She told them, pointing to her left. They looked and saw the earth covered with buffalo.

"Look this way she said," pointing partly behind her. Now, when they looked, they saw wide corn fields.

"Look that way,' she said once more and pointed to her right. This time they saw the prairie covered with horses.

"Look that way again," she told them. They looked and saw Indian fighting. Now they looked closer and saw themselves among the warriors, painted just as the old woman had painted them.

"You will always win in battle," she told them. "You will have good luck and take many captives."

And then she told them, "When you leave here go to the center of your village. Ask for two large bowls and have them wiped clean. Then say to your people, "We have something wonderful to give you." Tell your people that when the sun goes down, I will send out buffalo.'

She gave each of the young men some corn tied up in sacks and told them to divide this seed among their people. Finally, she told them to take some of the meat from the plate with one hand and some corn with the other hand. Then she sent them away. They left her lodge and came up out of the spring.

All of the people in the village were seated around the spring when they came out. The two young men went to the center of the camp and told the people what the old woman had said. Then they asked that two wooden bowls be brought to them, but these had to be clean. Then the young men put meat in one bowl and corn in the other. When they were finished, the bowls were filled.

The people began to eat, first the meat and then the corn. The old people ate first, then the younger men and women, and finally, the children. When they were finished, there was only a little meat and corn left. The last to eat were two orphans, a boy and a girl. By the time they were finished eating, there was nothing left.

As the sun went down, the people looked toward the spring. After a time, they saw a buffalo bull leap from the spring. He ran a short distance and pawed the ground, then he turned back and plunged back into the spring. Now suddenly, a great herd of buffalo ran from the spring. All night long the buffalo raced out of the spring, making such a noise that no one in the village could sleep.

The next morning, when the sun rose, there were buffalo as far as the eye could see. The hunters went out and brought in all the meat they could use.

The people camped there all winter and had plenty of food. Toward spring, they sent two young men out to find a damp place where they could plant corn, then made caches in the earth where they stored their dried meat. Finally they went off to plant corn, digging holes with sticks and planting the seed in the ground.

Every now and then they returned to get some more dried meat. Once, when they returned, they found that some of the seed had been taken, either by the Pawnees or the Arikarees. That is how those tribes got their corn.

It was Erect Horns (also known as Red Tassel or Standing on the Ground) who was responsible for bringing corn to the people. When he learned that they had been careless and had not kept watch over the corn, he took their power to raise corn from them

Some say that the other boy was Sweet Medicine (also known as Rustling Corn Leaf or Sweet Root Standing)

After that, the Cheyenne no longer planted corn but lived on the plains and hunted the buffalo

By Henry Tall Bull and Tom Weist Copyright 1972 by Montana Indian Publications (517 Rimrock Road, Billings, MT 59102) Reprinted with permission from the publisher

1 So taaeo o (Suhtaio) and Isetsehestahese (Tsistsistas) are the two historical divisions of the Cheyenne

2 A few versions of this story say that the swift-hawk, crow and eagle as well as the magpie, sided with the young man

3 "Old Womans Water" (Matamhe Hemapame) is an important legend for it contains an allegory of the joining of the So taaeo'o (Suhtaio) and Tsetsehestahese (Tsistsistas) into one tribe, hence the reason the boys are identically dressed In some versions both Erect Horns (Tomosevesehe) the So'taaeo'o (Suhtaio) culture hero and Sweet Medicine (Motse'eoeve), the culture hero of Tsetsehestahese (Tsistsistas) are named as the young men   Old Womans Water" (Matamaahe Hemapame) also tells of the change from growing corn and other vegetables to the Cheyennes' eventual movement onto the plains and their dependence upon the buffalo

4 Hoop or wheel game An old game played by the Cheyenne, it was most often played by throwing a stick with several prongs on the end at a rolling hoop The hoop was made of a stick tied together so it formed a circle this was interlaced with rawhide The object of the game was to strike the hoop in such a way that the stick stuck through the lacing thus counting as a kill '

Coming Home

I T WAS A cold, damp day Oct 16, 1993, when the Northern Cheyennes gathered to bury their dead near Busby, MT This memorial service was different
The procession leading across the high plains carried 18 cedar boxes Unlike
caskets, the boxes were short and nearly square Each contained a skull that had
been collected from a bloody trench in Nebraska and then spent the last century
in the Smithsonian Museum of Natural History cupboards in Washington, DC

James Black Wolf, Keeper of the Sacred Hat bundle that has been handed
down for nearly two centuries, prayed The sky filled with the soulful song of the
eagle-bone whistle Steve Little Bird, camp crier, called men from each warrior
society to bring the boxes into the sunlight the Crazy Dogs, the Elkhorn Scrapers, the Kit Foxes the Bowstrings Elkhorn Scraper Chief Gilbert White Dirt led
a song, his voice soaring as two young women started trilling to make the men's
hearts strong Then the crowd carried the boxes across U S Highway 212 to the
burial hill at the Chief Two Moons monument [1]

Burying the remains of these ancestors brought a mixture of anguish and
relief to the Northern Cheyennes who gathered there in 1993 They were forced
once again to confront the attitudes of the 19th century, when it was federal policy
to collect American Indian skulls United States Army Surgeon General Madison
Mills paid soldiers to ship skulls, saying, "Our collection of Indian crania, already
quite large, should be made as complete as possible " Government scientists wanted to measure the skulls to prove the superiority of the Caucasian race and thus
justify the policies of exterminating American Indians who stood in the way of
more "civilized" people [2] When Congress passed the Native American Graves Protection and Repatriation Act in 1990, there were believed to be more than 600,000
skeletal remains of American Indians in museums and private collections [3]

The relief came when the spirits expressed their gratitude for being brought
home, at long last The three-year-old girl who was being freed from her imprison-

Many tears were shed when the remains of Northern Cheyennes killed at Fort Robinson finally came home to rest, 115 years after they began their journey from Indian Territory. Pictured are the cedar boxes containing the remains and the holes where they were buried. (Photo by John Warner)

ment at the Smithsonian appeared to a young man there He saw her dressed in white with yellow ribbons in her hair, and she was happy After the wake at Busby, a small teddy bear was given to the little girl and placed on the cedar box with her remains [4] In route from Washington to Busby, the delegation stopped at Fort Robinson, NE, and held a pipe ceremony At dawn an old lady started crying The delegation could not see her, but at the end of the prayer, they heard her say, "*Nea'esemeno*" ("thank you" in Cheyenne) [5]

It had been a long journey home for the little girl, the old woman, and the others who arrived back at Busby While often referred to as the fighting Cheyenne, they were fighters by necessity, not choice, according to Tom Weist in his book, *A History of the Cheyenne People* [6] The tribe stood on the brink of extinction several times, threatened not only by soldiers' guns but just as often by government neglect when promised rations never arrived They fought their way back, sometimes armed only by knives, empty rifles, determination, and the strong hearts of their women

The Fort Laramie Treaty of 1851 assigned a vast territory of the Northern Plains east of the Rocky Mountains to the Cheyenne and Arapahoe tribes In 1868, some of the Cheyennes and Lakota signed a treaty creating the Great Sioux Reservation, which encompassed much of the present states of Montana, Wyoming, Nebraska, and portions of the Dakotas The treaty said "No white person should be permitted to settle or to pass through the same [area] without the consent of the Indians first "[7]

However, neither side abided by the treaty After gold was discovered in the Black Hills in 1872, the government changed the rules All Indians were ordered to reservations, and troops were sent out to round them up Then on June 26 1876 the Cheyennes, Arapahos, Lakota, and other allies defeated Custer (25 miles west of Busby) Custer and 264 of his men were killed [8] After the victory, the United States and the American public forgot about treaties and thirsted for vengeance

SOUTH TO INDIAN TERRITORY

In the summer of 1877 , Chiefs Dull Knife[9] and Little Wolf and 970 other Cheyennes were taken south to Indian Territory to live with the Southern Cheyennes at the Darlington Agency Promised food and a new life, they reluctantly agreed to move An attack on the Dull Knife camp the previous November had destroyed their lodges, their winter food supply, all their belongings, and their morale

Accustomed to an active life on the high, dry plains and mountains and plentiful game, they did not adjust well to the hot, muggy climate in Indian Territory where there were inadequate rations, and the game had been exterminated The agent there knew that they were not being treated fairly He testified before a committee of the Senate that he never received supplies to feed the Indians for more than nine months a year "These people were meat-eaters, but the beef furnished them by the government inspectors was no more than skin and bone," he said The agent described their suffering "They have lived, and that is about all "[10] In truth, a lot did not live The malnourished people got malaria and measles, and the agency physician could not treat all the sick Many children and old people died After they had endured the conditions for a year, Chiefs Dull Knife and Little Wolf went to see the Indian agent, John D Miles Little Wolf said,

> We have come to ask the agent that we be sent home to our own country in the mountains My people were raised there, in a land of pines and clear, cold rivers There, we were always healthy for there was meat enough for all this is not a good place for us Before another year has passed, we may all be dead, and there will be none of us left to travel north [11]

Miles, a Quaker, could see the suffering of the Cheyennes, but he had his orders from Washington The Northern Cheyennes were to remain in the south Little Wolf told his people what Miles had said Some wanted to go, others wanted to stay rather than be hunted down and killed Little Wolf went back to Miles and said,

> Listen, my friends, I am a friend of the white people and have been so for a long time I do not want to see blood spilt about this agency I am going north to my own country If you are going to send your soldiers after me, I wish you would let us get a little distance away Then if you want to fight, I will fight you, and we can make the ground bloody at that place [12]

Knowing that they faced a hazardous trek of over 1,500 miles with women, children, and old people weakened by hunger and disease, 297 Cheyennes rose in the early morning hours of Sept 9, 1878, and started north, many of them on foot, leaving the bodies of their loved ones and most of their belongings behind [13] *Isehne'evahoohtoosemevose Tsetsehestahese*, they were going home Their route was not through wilderness but through hazardous areas occupied by homesteaders and ranchers and crossed by several railroads, which could carry troops

Exile and Escape

The Northern Cheyennes succeeded in escaping Indian Territory, but they paid a big price In his book, *Tell Them We Are Going Home The Odyssey of the Northern Cheyennes*, John Monnett says that the exodus of the Cheyennes was equally as important as the heroic flight of the Nez Perce under Chief Joseph He credited brilliant military maneuvers for their escape from Indian Territory However, some of the Cheyenne people have another explanation Some say they relied on their sacred cultural ways to sustain them An old medicine woman by the

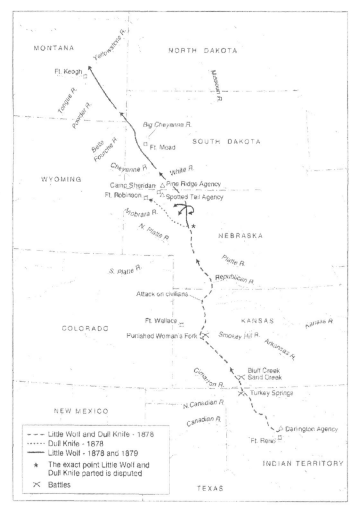

When they escaped from Indian Territory to return to Montana, the Northern Cheyennes traveled over 1,500 miles under pursuit by government soldiers. Their party included women, children, and old people weakened by hunger and disease. No one thought they could do it. Author John Monnett credited their brilliant military maneuvers. Some of the Cheyennes credited Notame'hehe (Northern Woman), who turned the people into small herds of buffalo when the soldiers came near. (Map courtesy of University of Oklahoma Press)

name of *Notame'hehe* (North Woman) divined the route for them By using sacred ceremonies, she told the people what to do and, using the powers of *Heseeota'e*, she hid them The soldiers thought they were small herds of buffalo when they came close to finding them [14]

One of the women, Susan Iron Teeth, said, "We dodged the soldiers during most of the way But they were always near us and trying to catch us Our young men fought them off in seven different battles At each fight, some of our people were killed, women or children the same as men I do not know how many of our grown-up people were killed But I know that more than 60 of our children were gone when we got to the Dakota country "[15]

As fall turned into winter, their moccasins wore out from six weeks of walking Some wrapped their feet in rags to get through the snow Many suffered from dysentery Some of the young Cheyenne warriors, angry and desperately needing horses and supplies, attacked white settlers in western Kansas and Nebraska, killing over 40 and raping several women, according to Monnett's documentation [16]

When they reached the Platte River, the group split up Little Wolf's band camped to wait out the winter on the Lost Chokecherry Creek before proceeding to the Tongue River country The other band led by Dull Knife moved to the northwest, hoping to find refuge with the Lakota at Red Cloud Agency in Nebraska The 149 followers that decided to join Dull Knife were mostly women, children, elderly, and a few warriors [17]

FORT ROBINSON BREAKOUT (*TSEXHOVA'XEVÓSE TSÉTSEHESTAHESE*)

On Oct 23, 1878, Dull Knife's band encountered soldiers in a snowstorm in the Nebraska Sandhills who told them that their goal—Red Cloud Agency—had been moved north to Dakota Territory [18] The Cheyenne were so desperate for food and shelter that they went to Fort Robinson with the soldiers Among the prisoners taken to Fort Robinson were Iron Teeth and her children and the artist Little Finger Nail Little Finger Nail had his ledger book of drawings strapped on his back, concealed under his clothing The ledger book contained drawings from their trek from Indian Territory to Fort Robinson [19]

Iron Teeth lived another 50 years until May 1928, and she described the tragic events to Thomas D Marquis, a local physician and historian Iron Teeth was an experienced hunter and a good rider who in happier days had broken her own horses Women normally did not hunt and were expected to tend to lodge keeping, tanning, food preparation, and childrearing However, a few women participated in buffalo hunts and fought alongside the men in battle These women were referred to as Manly-Hearted Women The Northern Cheyenne community fully accepted these women

Initially, Dull Knife and his followers had limited freedom to hunt near Fort Robinson, and they tried to nourish hope of reuniting with the other Cheyennes and Lakota in the north. Later, however, they were locked in the barracks. In a room that measured about 30 feet square there were 43 men, 29 women, and 20 to 30 children.[20]

On Jan. 3, 1879, they heard the news that they had been dreading for two months. The Indian Bureau in Washington had ordered that they be taken back to Indian Territory. When they refused, Captain Henry W. Wessells, Jr., the commanding officer, cut off all food and firewood despite the bitter cold—temperatures had dropped well below zero. Then Wessells cut off all water for three days, fully expecting them to give in and agree to go to Indian Territory.

Wessells had not counted on the determination of the Cheyennes. They scraped frost off the windows for water and planned their next desperate move. After watching so many of their family and friends die horrible deaths, the Cheyenne men and women felt they had nothing left to lose. Iron Teeth and the other women were preparing for the escape or for death. They had hidden rifles under the floorboards of the barracks, and men armed themselves with the women's household knives. Iron Teeth had concealed a revolver under the bodice of her dress for her son, Gathering His Medicine, 22, to use.[21]

Late on the night of Jan. 9, they made their break. Gathering His Medicine and the others smashed windows and tore the door down. Gathering His Medicine put his youngest sister on his back and ran in one direction while Iron Teeth and another daughter ran the other way. Cheyenne women, some carrying children, fought soldiers.[22]

In an interview with Marquis dated 1926 Iron Teeth stated:

> We stayed in the cave seven nights and almost seven days. More snow kept falling. It was very cold, but we were afraid to build a fire. We nibbled at my small store of dry meat and melted snow for water. Each day we could hear the horses and the voices of soldiers searching for Indians. Finally a soldier found our tracks, and the soldiers then took us back to Fort Robinson.[23]

More than 30 were trapped in a washout at Antelope Creek, 35 miles from Fort Robinson. Troopers fired into the pit for three-quarters of an hour. Then they charged, firing their weapons, withdrawing and reloading and charging until the death songs were silent. Suddenly three bleeding young men leaped from the pit with knives and empty guns, and they were killed, too. One mortally wounded woman who had slit her daughter's throat to keep her from being captured was still alive when a lieutenant reached down to comfort her. She spat in his face.[24]

In all about 60 people were killed after the Fort Robinson break out, including Little Finger Nail. The bullets that ripped through his body also ripped his ledger.[25] After being imprisoned again at Fort Robinson, Iron Teeth was afraid to ask anybody about her son and the little daughter, fearing that by asking, she would inform the soldiers of them. "After a while the little girl came to me. I asked her about her brother. It appeared she did not hear me, so I asked again. This time she burst out crying. Then I knew he had been killed," she told Marquis.[26]

The Northern Cheyenne odyssey was widely covered by the press at the time and led to severe public criticism of the military. When several Cheyenne leaders were put on trial for killing the white settlers, they were acquitted, partially because of public sympathy. While the survivors expected to be shot or sent back to Indian Territory, most were taken to Pine Ridge Agency to live with the Oglala Lakota. For some time, it was thought that Dull Knife had been killed.[27] However, he and his wife, and their son Bull Hump were separated from the main body of Cheyennes, and they reached Pine Ridge Agency several weeks later.

Meanwhile, after waiting out the winter of 1878-1879 on the Lost Chokecherry, Little Wolf was persuaded by Cheyenne emissaries to surrender at Fort Keogh on March 26, 1879. Dull Knife and the other survivors from his band joined them in November. Once again, the government had placed too many Indians in too small of an area, and there was not enough grass for horses, farming land, or game. Gen. Nelson A. Miles later let certain Cheyennes leave Fort Keogh and hunt up the Tongue River where they eventually settled with their families near Lame Deer and Muddy creeks. Other Cheyennes settled near Rosebud Creek.[28]

TONGUE RIVER INDIAN RESERVATION

By this time, most of the tribes in the West had reservations, and Congress had ended the treaty-making era in 1871. Reservations could only be established by direct order of the president of the United States. The Tongue River Indian Reservation was created by Executive Order under President Chester A. Arthur on Nov. 16, 1884. The reservation consisted of 371,200 acres.[29] Dull Knife, who sacrificed so much to lead his people back to the north, died in 1883, the year before the reservation was established. He was originally buried on a high butte overlooking Rosebud Creek, approximately eight miles west of Lame Deer, but he was moved to Lame Deer.

This 1884 reservation boundary excluded many Cheyennes who lived east of the river where they had been encouraged to homestead. Those who lived outside the reservation could not get government services, so the new St. Labre's Catholic Mission dispensed medicine and other aid. Partly at the insistence of the bishop, the governor wired the Secretary of Interior for assistance for them. In March 19, 1900, the reservation was increased to 444,157 acres by Executive Order under President William McKinley, and these homesteads were included within the new boundary.[30]

Chiefs Dull Knife and Little Wolf led the Northern Cheyenne people on their long trip home from Indian Territory, a heroic journey immortalized in the novel *Cheyenne Autumn* by Mari Sandoz. Little Wolf (standing) wears what appears to be a cross, but it actually represents the dragonfly, an important religious symbol.

While many white citizens of the county still tried to have the Northern Cheyennes removed and their reservation dissolved, the Cheyennes also had many white allies, including the Catholic mission, some area families, and some government officials who said they should remain on the Tongue River Reservation undisturbed One of the letters was from Gen Miles dated June 1889 " in regard to the proposed removal of the Indians [Northern Cheyenne], there is no good reason or justice in doing so They have fulfilled their part of the compact [to remain at peace], they have an undoubted right, legally and morally, to remain where they are now located [31]

Conclusion

Recent research has revealed that American Indian people are still experiencing the trauma of their ancestors Problems of alcoholism, drug abuse, suicide, and mental illness may be symptoms of historic trauma However, the research also indicates that revitalizing cultural and spiritual ceremonies can help people heal [32]

For the last several years, the Northern Cheyennes remember the great odyssey of their ancestors with the Fort Robinson Break Out Spiritual Run each January The first run involved nine descendants who ran a 76-mile loop around the Northern Cheyenne Reservation In 1999 they began making the full 400-mile run from Fort Robinson through the Black Hills to the reservation in Montana The annual event is primarily a ceremonial run to honor the ancestors It also brings youth and adults together, teaches history and culture, and creates a bond amongst family, youth, and elders [33]

1 Giarelli A L (1993 Nov 15) The return of the Cheyenne skulls brings a bloody Western story to a close *High Country News* 25(21)

2 Gulliford, A (Fall 1996) Bones of contention The repatriation of Native American human remains *The Public Historian, 18*(4) 1-2

3 Thornton R , (1998) Who owns our past? The Repatriation of Native American Human Remains and Cultural Objects In R Thornton (Ed), *Studying Native America problems and prospects* (p 387) Madison University of Wisconsin Press

4 Thornton, Who owns our past? p 386

5 Giarelli, The return of the Cheyenne skulls

6 Weist, T (1977) *A history of the Cheyenne people* (p 6) Billings Montana Council for Indian Education

7 Weist, T (1977) *A history of the Cheyenne people* (p 68)

8 Weist, I (1977) *A history of the Cheyenne people* (p 76)

9 Dull Knife is a Sioux name, but among the Northern Cheyenne, he is known as *Voohehá ta* (Morning Star)

10 Eastman, C A (n d) Little Wolf In e-book, *Indian Heroes and Great Chieftains* (Dover Publications, 1997) Retrieved 12/15/07 from http //www authorama com/indian-heroes-and-great-chieftains-14 html Eastman cites anthropologist Grinnell G (1956) *The Fighting Cheyennes* Norman University of Oklahoma Press

11 Weist, I (1977) *A history of the Cheyenne people* (p 80)

12 Eastman, Little Wolf

13 Weist, *A history of the Cheyenne people* (p 80)

14 Bureau of Land Management, Department of Interior (Jan 2003) *Final statewide oil and gas environmental impact statement Northern Cheyenne narrative report* (pp 2-16) Retrieved Dec 2007 from http //www mt blm gov/mclo/cbm/eis/ NCheyenneNarrativeReport/Chap2 pdf

15 Marquis, T (1978) *The Cheyennes of Montana* Algonac MI Reference Publications, Inc

16 Monnett, J (2001) *Tell them we are going home* Norman Oklahoma University of Oklahoma Press

17 Monnett, *Tell them we are going home*

18 Weist, *A history of the Cheyenne people* (p 81)

19 Low, D (Summer 2006) Composite Indigenous genre Cheyenne ledger art as literature *Studies in American Indian Literature (18)*2 83-104 Lincoln University of Nebraska Press Retrieved Dec 12 2007, from http //ezproxy twu edu 2122/journals/ studies_in_american_indian_lit html

20 Monnett, *Tell them we are going home*

21 Marquis, *The Cheyennes of Montana*

22 Monnett, *Tell them we are going home*

23 Marquis *The Cheyennes of Montana* (p 77)

24 Giarelli 1 he return of the Cheyenne skulls 1 he skulls repatriated in 1993 came from the Antelope Creek mass grave

25 Low, Composite Indigenous genre Cheyenne ledger art Soldiers gave the book to an Army officer, Francis Hardie, as a war souvenir The ledger is now on display at the Natural History Museum in New York City

26 Marquis, *The Cheyennes of Montana* (p 77)

27 Charles Eastmans story, for example mistakenly says that Dull Knife was killed there at Fort Robinson

28 Weist, *A history of the Cheyenne people* (p 103)

29 Weist *A history of the Cheyenne people* (p 104)

30 Weist, *A history of the Cheyenne people* (p 106-107)

31 Bureau of Land Management, *Final statewide oil and gas environmental impact statement*

32 Yellow Horse Brave Heart, M & Deschenie, T (Winter 2006) Historical trauma and post colonial stress in American Indian populations *Tribal College Journal 17*(3)

33 Melmer, D (2006, Jan 13) Dull Knife run honors ancestors and youth *Indian Country Today*

The Northern Cheyenne Language

I T IS A fact of indigenous lives that languages are dying These deaths have been extensively documented To write more about it seems to be giving in to the unspoken consensus that indigenous languages are indeed going to die Yet, the prospect of their deaths must be discussed by indigenous people because only we can save them—only we value them is living, sacred beings

Perhaps languages have built-in obsolescence based on the very fact that they, too, are alive They, too, die after they have served their purposes For those who speak a dying language, language death can be an event as horrific as that comet that, theoretically, killed the dinosaurs 65 million years ago, or it can be almost a non-event, as described in the article, "The Death of Language," by linguist David Crystal "A language dies only when the last person who speaks it dies One day it is there, the next it is gone "[1]

For the Cheyenne language in Montana, the time of its potential death can almost be pinpointed In 1996, an informal survey was conducted to find the youngest fluent speaker The survey was not scientifically done, there were no comparison groups, no systematic approach, and no longitudinal observations Only those volunteers willing to be tape recorded were included Speakers were recorded for half an hour The only speaker who could sustain Cheyenne speech for half an hour, and who probably could have gone on much longer, was Rhoda Glenmore This 45-year-old lady is now (2007) about 56 years of age

So, it could be predicted that the Cheyenne language's viability could coincide with the possible life span of this speaker If she lived to be 85, it would be the year 2036, and she could be the only living Native speaker alive at that time She would have no one to talk to in Cheyenne She would talk Cheyenne, but there would be no receptive ears or comprehending brains anywhere in the world She would be speaking only to herself The area around her would be filling rapidly with the noises of non-indigenous tongues

This language has a long history, and the Cheyenne people have many reasons to keep it alive. We have taken several steps to invigorate it. However, we also have many obstacles.

HISTORY OF THE CHEYENNE LANGUAGE

Tsesenestsestotse, the Cheyenne language, is an Algonquian language, a group that also includes Arapaho, Blackfeet, Cree, Delaware, Fox, Mohegan, Ojibwa, Ottawa, Potawatomi, Kickapoo, Menominee, Fox, Sac, Shawnee, Micmac, and Naskapi. It is one of the westernmost Algonquian languages. It changed to its present spoken and written form when two very similar languages combined—the Cheyenne language proper and the *So'taahe* language. Perhaps as early as the 1900s these two once-distinctly identifiable languages merged to such an extent that they were effectively one language, according to George Bird Grinnell.[2]

The Cheyenne language has been written since 1896 when the Reverend Rodolphe Petter, a Mennonite missionary, wrote and published the first Cheyenne language dictionary. He also designed the alphabet when he began to study the Cheyenne language in Oklahoma at the end of the 19th century. This alphabet has 14 letters, which combine to create long words that are comprised of many smaller meaning parts. This alphabet fits the sounds and patterns of the Cheyenne language very well.

The letter "z" was used in the Petter alphabet to represent the "ts" sound, because Petter spoke German, which uses the letter "z" for that sound. In the early 1970s, a Cheyenne committee working with linguist Danny Alford and the bilingual education program in the Lame Deer, MT, schools, changed the "z" to the two English letters "ts." This alphabet can be called the Petter Alphabet, or Modified Petter Alphabet.[3]

Since these early efforts, the writing system has undergone progressively more understandable changes. On April 21, 1997, the Northern Cheyenne Tribal Council took a significant step. It passed an ordinance declaring Cheyenne as the official language of the tribe.[4]

In 1997 Wayne Leman created a Cheyenne language website (www.geocities.com/cheyenne_language/alphabet.htm) that provides the alphabet, a pronunciation guide, online access to the Cheyenne Dictionary, and reference materials. Leman is an SIL linguist who lived with the Northern Cheyenne in Montana for about 35 years. He and his wife now live in Spokane. (Founded over 70 years ago, SIL International is a faith-based organization that studies, documents, and assists in developing the world's lesser-known languages.)

Some other tribes have put their languages into writing only reluctantly because members believed that they should only be spoken. However, there has been little controversy amongst the Cheyenne concerning the writing system. Occasionally there are moves to change this writing system, instigated by people who have minimal understanding of linguistics systems and conventions.

Languages change and adjust to changing times and differing social phenomena. In some cases, the pronunciation changes. For example, the Cheyenne world is divided into animacy and inanimacy so indicators for these classifications become very important in Cheyenne talking, reading, and writing. *He'tohe* is the indicator for inanimacy, and the present older generation (50 years and older) says it this way. The younger generation (50 and younger) adds another glottal stop just before the last voiceless *e (he'to'e)*. This change does not impede clarity or communication, but it does rattle the nerves of Cheyenne purists. In other cases, the meaning changes. For example, *tosa'e nevee'e* means "where are you camped?" However, the younger generation uses *tosa'e nevee'e?* When they're really asking *tosa'e nevo'ostaneheve* which means "where do you live?"

The Cheyennes were one of the Algonquian-speaking peoples who were believed to have traditionally inhabited this area of North America hundreds of years ago. (Map reprinted from *A History of the Cheyenne People* with permission from the publisher)

The Cheyenne seem to have quit devising new words for the changing times and emerging social phenomena in the late 1950s. There are words for automobile, airplane, influenza, cancer, and movies. Then this coining of new words abruptly ended in the 1960s, we have no words for hippies, radar, sonar, flying saucers, HIV, or football. As a Cheyenne language teacher, I was asked to translate "ketchup." After some thought, I called it "tomato gravy" since we had the word for tomato *heneno'e* and the word for gravy *enahano*, I just combined the two words to make an acceptable-sounding Cheyenne word *heneneenahano* Then I was asked to translate "mustard." I translated it to *me'e'sekevotseenahano*—'baby gravy," which I think is self-explanatory.

The development of the Cheyenne dictionary has been a major contribution to the continued viability of the Cheyenne language. The contributions of linguists like Rodolphe Petter, Dan Alford, and Wayne Leman have made the talking and teaching of the Cheyenne language much easier. Dictionaries of the Cheyenne language have helped to preserve the language even as some of the cultural artifacts (like "corn ceremonies") on which the words were based have become obsolete.

However, dictionaries by themselves cannot save a language as a spoken language. They must be used primarily as resources for teaching, for writing, for standardizing the language so that reading materials can be constructed with uniform standards that are universally applicable for Cheyenne and non-Cheyenne people. It is unfortunate to have to apply these strictures to a dynamic language and render it static. Since the Cheyenne language is rapidly becoming a classroom subject, some uniformity is needed for testing, reading, and writing purposes.

SAVING THE SPOKEN LANGUAGE

Today, there are efforts to save the language at Chief Dull Knife College and at local school districts, and one immersion school is being contemplated in the Lame Deer area. Chief Dull Knife College has a three-year Administration for Native American grant designed to teach Cheyenne speakers how to read, write, and produce curriculum or other written material. At least 13 people are learning how to do those three things, but the grant is in its last year.

Chief Dull Knife College administers a Class 7 licensure program on behalf of the tribe. It is now part of the Montana state teacher certification process for language and culture teachers. Each Montana tribal group qualifies its own language and culture teachers, and the state certifies those teachers. It is a progressive and innovative concept now being copied by other surrounding states.[5] One Class 7 teacher, Mabel Kills Night, is teaching the Cheyenne language via the internet to Colstrip High School students and is very successful. The college plans to expand this program to three other schools in 2008.

Cheyenne Immersion Camp Instructor Patty Oldman asked students to identify animals in Cheyenne. (Photo by Conrad Fisher)

Students learned to dry meat at the Cheyenne Immersion Camp. (Photo by Conrad Fisher)

The Northern Cheyenne Language

For many years, the tribal college has sponsored Cheyenne language immersion camps during the summer, which have been very successful and always much anticipated by Cheyenne youth

WHY KEEP IT ALIVE

Cheyenne people do not want our language to die, but there are many obstacles to saving it One is the lack of funding Another is the lack of understanding Why would a small tribe of people want to perpetuate a language that the larger population around us does not care about?

It is difficult to defend to the non-Cheyenne world the continued existence of the Cheyenne language because it has to be defended in the abstract parameters of what the language means to Cheyenne people individually and culturally Cheyenne people know intrinsically that the Cheyenne language is as relevant as any other language on this planet We do not measure the relevance of our language against the number of people who speak it but by the communal, spiritual, and communicative relevance it has to us This relevance to Cheyenne people, as trite as it may sound, is what makes the Cheyenne language so important to us

Furthermore, the Cheyenne language is difficult to defend because the arguments against it are couched in economic, academic, sociologic, linguistic, and stereotypical terms—terms that contain what the majority society deems important The debate against the Cheyenne language is measured in terms that have little or no relevance to Cheyenne speakers " but Cheyenne is not spoken at the forums of the United Nations ", " but Cheyenne is not spoken in the United States Congress ", " but Cheyenne is not spoken in the state legislature ", " but the Cheyenne language is not spoken even in our own tribal council deliberations " These are all logical arguments—on the surface

The reasons that make the Cheyenne language relevant to Cheyenne people lie below the surface deep down in the collective Cheyenne psyche and spirit Perhaps this language can help unite or re-unite the Cheyenne people and bring us back into balance and harmony with each other and lead to the elimination of the many issues that divide and hamper us Perhaps, the Northern Cheyennes can use the language to settle divisive issues and issues that are subconsciously presenting barriers

GRIEF AND MOURNING

We observe the grieving processes all too frequently on the Cheyenne reservation Perhaps some of these deaths can be blamed upon our loss of land and language

It should be easy, now to understand the destitution of indigenous, oral persons who have been forcibly displaced from their traditional lands. The local earth is, for them, the very matrix of discursive meaning, to force them from their native ecology (for whatever political or economic purpose) is to render them speech-less—or to render their speech meaningless—to *dislodge them from the very ground of coherence*. It is quite simply, to force them out of their mind. The massive 'relocation' or "transmigration" projects underway in numerous parts of the world today in the name of "progress"   must be understood, in this light, as instances of cultural genocide [6]

David Abram argues that relocating and confining Cheyennes on a reservation in effect dislodged us from "the very ground of coherence" It forced us out of our minds. It is going to take time to recover this "ground of coherence" and to regain the right frame of mind. The Cheyenne language must play an influential role in this recovery

The Northern Cheyennes are experiencing difficult times with the present world possibly because we have experienced huge losses of language, spirituality, land, and loved ones. The Cheyenne people who inhabit the skid rows and jails of this country are there, indirectly, because of the grieving they feel but may not be adequately able to articulate in either the English language or in the Cheyenne language. They do not have the vocabulary in either language to express their emotional and spiritual pain. This inability to articulate pain leads to rage that either needs to be vented or suppressed. Either alternative is dysfunctional because vented rage can lead to considerable harm to one's loved ones or to one's self. Suppressed rage can lead to self-sedation with drugs or alcohol.

Making this connection might be a reach. Using the Cheyenne language to revive healthy relationships is reason enough to maintain the Cheyenne language. It is difficult to regain healthy relations in today's society because of the change of the family make-up and because of negative external forces like the following

> Traditionally, extended families live in close proximity. Grandparents, aunts, and uncles play important roles in each child's upbringing. And as parents and grandparents age, they expect the support of younger generations. Yet a lack of jobs on the reservation often means young people must leave for work. Furthermore the very concept of institutional education harbors painful connotations for many of the grandparents so integral in the lives of Cheyenne kids. When today's elders were children, the government was still forcing kids to go to boarding schools, where they were punished for speaking their own language. Family involvement in education is key, and we cannot get families involved

Identity: Individual and Cultural

Native speakers believe that language and identity are closely tied. Embedded in this language are the lessons that guide our daily lives. We cannot leave behind the essence of our being. As Hualapai educator Lucille Jackson Watahomigie expresses it, "It is said that when the languages were created, language identified the people—who we are, where we came from, and where we are going." Navajo artist and educator Fred Bia said, "My language, to me ....that's what makes me unique, that's what makes me Navajo, that's what makes me who I am." William Harjo Lonefight said, "When people spoke Dakota, they understood where they belonged in relation to other people, to the natural world, and to the spiritual world."[8]

Assimilationist education denied Cheyennes the right to speak our own language, and the foundation of a healthy individual identity was severely shaken. We were denied the ability to speak Cheyenne and forced to take on a persona other than the one ensconced in and identified by the Cheyenne language. It was bound to fail, and fail it did simply because so many Cheyennes were not able to speak English even if they were willing to deny their Cheyenne-ness. This shake-up reverberated until it had reached every nook and cranny of the Cheyenne culture, and this culture is still experiencing aftershock after aftershock in academics, economics, spirituality, and socially.

In 1975, Dillon Platero, the first director of the Navajo Division of Education, described the experience of "Kee," a Navajo student who became nonlingual. Kee's story illustrates what happened and still happening to many Cheyennes:

> Kee was sent to boarding school as a child where—as was the practice—he was punished for speaking Navajo. Since he was only allowed to return home during Christmas and summers, he lost contact with his family. Kee withdrew from both the White and Navajo worlds as he grew older because he could not comfortably communicate in either language. He became one of the many thousands of Navajos who were nonlingual—a man with out a language. By the time he was 16, Kee was an alcoholic, uneducated, and despondent—without identity.[9]

Thus a byproduct of the denial of speaking tribal languages was spawned, the drunken, lazy Indian stereotype. Stereotypes have had devastating effects on all American Indians, and these stereotypes continue to exact tolls from individuals.

STEREOTYPES

Many writings have oversimplified Northern Cheyenne culture and have, perhaps unwittingly, contributed to the stereotypes of Native cultures that pervade U.S. society and the world. These stereotypes and oversimplifications contribute not only to misinformation and myth within the larger culture but also function as economic and social oppressors to living American Indians.

Bently Spang, a Cheyenne artist who lives in Billings, MT, speaks and writes often about stereotypes. If most citizens of the United States see American Indians only as cartoons like the mascot of the Atlanta Braves and Cleveland Indians "Chief Wahoo," who will hire a American Indian so that he or she can support their families in a meaningful way? he asks. If the American Indians are seen only as mystics and shamans who are not of this earth, then American Indians obviously require no earthly sustenance to support themselves or their children, he argues.

Spang points out that American Indians are not a hobby, a fascination, a retail item, a breed to be authenticated to facilitate economic consumption of their historical artifacts, a nameless dancing Indian on a travel brochure or a U S version of the classic Greek tragedy. American Indians represent complex, living cultures with their own body of knowledge and the capability to express and document their own histories in this and all other time periods.

The following quotes further buttress the harm that stereotypes do to Cheyenne people and to all American Indians.

> A phenomenon in White culture affects any interaction between White people and Native Americans. White culture has created an image and called it "Indian." But this image is a stereotype and not really informative or accurate about real Native Americans, who are of many diverse cultures. All of us could give details about this stereotype "Indian." An important aspect of this stereotype "Indian" is that it has two sides, like the two sides of a coin.
>
> One side of the stereotype Indian is the Hostile Savage—the dangerous, primitive warrior who attacked the settlers of the West, or the irresponsible reservation drunk who couldn't be trusted, the Indian of which it was said, "the only good Indian is a dead Indian." The other side of the stereotype Indian is the Noble Savage—the innocent primitive who was naturally spiritual and lived in idyllic harmony close to the earth, the Indian of the Thanksgiving stories who helped the Pilgrims survive. These images are embedded deeply in our culture and are subliminal backdrop to any of our interactions with Native people or concepts"[10]

Stereotypes have instilled cultural and self-hatred among Cheyenne people, especially young people. American Indians must be proactive in doing away with stereotypes imposed by the white society. Speaking the Cheyenne language can help instill a more positive self-image among the Cheyenne people.

RECOMMENDATIONS

After the 1996 survey, Rhoda Glenmore was said to be the youngest fluent speaker. Since that time, several younger Cheyenne speakers have told her they could speak the language. She believes she served as a catalyst for making people aware of how important it is to speak the language Whether or not there is more than one speaker under the age of 56 today, we know that its viability depends upon all of us

Cheyennes should do the same things for our language as we are doing for the English language become both fluent (being able to sustain a prolonged conversation with fellow Cheyenne speakers) and literate (being able to read and write the Cheyenne language) These are crucial skills that are needed to transfer the language and the culture to coming generations

If present-day Cheyennes do not attempt to acquire these two skills, then we are indirectly depriving our descendants of the opportunity to speak, hear, read, and write Cheyenne No generation wants to be last to speak the Cheyenne language fluently, we do not want to be the generation that stops the flow of the Cheyenne language forever These skills are needed so that Cheyennes can produce our own written literature—poetry, short stories, novels, plays and movie scripts utilizing both ancient oral literature and contemporary events

Being fluent in the Cheyenne language is the first requirement for a successful language teacher However, it takes more than fluency to teach any language and Cheyenne is no exception Since Cheyenne is now being taught in classrooms, it is imperative that Cheyenne language teachers learn teaching methods, learn about second language acquisition principles, learn lesson planning and curriculum development, and acquire classroom management skills Cheyenne language and culture teachers owe it to the Cheyenne language to make a supreme effort to learn all about our language and culture, and that takes effort, application, and persistence

Cheyenne language teachers should join the efforts aimed at perpetuating the Cheyenne language in Montana and Oklahoma Cheyenne language teachers however, need to go beyond curricular, school-related issues The Cheyenne language was never meant to be taught in classrooms, it was meant to be passed on through the family, and that is the venue to which it should return

That should be the ideal, the goal for all language programs to rescue Cheyenne from the classroom and put it back in the family To do that means going beyond personal and political issues Squabbling about minor details of the language is not going to help perpetuate it In fact, more of the elders are going to travel on while this is happening Besides, adults present poor role models when they argue with each other

Conclusion

What does the Cheyenne language mean to Cheyenne people? It transmits all aspects of the Cheyenne culture If the whole tribe could get together to save the language, a collateral effect would be to show the outside world that we are capable of acting in a unified way, as we did in the grueling trek north from Oklahoma There could be a better understanding of Cheyenne spirituality, which embodies a reverence for all living and non-living things It could also help us to better understand the spirituality of those Cheyenne people who have embraced organized, non-traditional forms of worship

The Cheyenne language is a sacred language It conveys the minutest essence of sacred ceremonies with highly specialized language that is privy only to those select few who have undergone rigorous and demanding Cheyenne rituals This specialized language with its specific references can only be used by certain qualified people, male and female, in certain rituals Yet like all aspects of this Cheyenne language, these special terms are rapidly disappearing, succumbing to human mortality Somehow, this specialized language and references have to be saved, but only the headsmen and leaders of these groups can do that

Two languages comprise the present day Cheyenne language Over time the So'taahe and Cheyenne languages have co-existed in complementary and supplementary fashion to enrich Cheyenne life and spirituality Present day Cheyennes should take that as the supreme object lesson of unity

1 Crystal, D (Nov 1999) Millennium briefing The death of language *Prospect* 46 Available online http //www prospect-magazine co uk/

2 Grinnell, G B (1923) *The Cheyenne Indians Their history and ways of life, Vol 1* (pp 9-10) New Haven, CT Yale University Press

3 http //www.geocities com/cheyenne_language/alphabet htm Retrieved Dec 2007

4 http //www geocities com/cheyenne_language/alphabet htm Retrieved Dec 2007

5 Rathbun, S D (Summer 2003) Language teacher found learning to be healing. *Tribal College Journal* 14(4) Available online www tribalcollegejournal org

6 Abram, D (1996) *The spell of the sensuous Perception and language in a more-than-human world* (p 178) New York Vintage Books

7 Franz, Z (2006) Skipping out & missing out Truancy takes its toll *Indian Education A Special Report* Missoula, MT University of Montana School of Journalism Available online http //www umt edu/journalism/student_work/Native News 2006/story_ncheyenne html

8 McCarty, T L Romero, M E , & Zepeda, O (2006) Reclaiming the gift Indigenous youth counter-narratives on Native language loss and revitalization *American Indian Quarterly* 30(1-2). 28-48 Lincoln University of Nebraska Press

9 Reyhner J (Nov/Dec , 2005) Cultural rights, language revival, and individual healing *Language Learner Magazine*, 22-23 Washington DC National Association for Bilingual Education Available online http //jan ucc nau edu/~jar/l Lcultural html

10 Johnson M (April 1995) Wanting to be Indian When spiritual searching turns into cultural theft *The Brown Papers* 1(7) Boston Women's Theological Center

Northern Cheyenne Reservation District Names

THE TONGUE RIVER Indian Reservation was created by Executive Order under President Chester A Arthur on Nov 16, 1884 The reservation consisted of 371,200 acres [1] On March 19, 1900, the reservation was increased to 444,157 acres by Executive Order under President William McKinley Within the second Executive Order, the reservation was referred to as the Northern Cheyenne Indian Reservation, replacing the earlier Tongue River Indian Reservation name The eastern boundary of the reservation was established as the mid stream of the Tongue River [2]

There are five official districts on the reservation now Both the Cheyenne and English names of the districts have many stories of their origins and there is much discussion about which version is true The reservation also contains some areas that are not officially recognized as political districts, but they have a history of their own Other areas are also being developed Clusters of homes are springing up south of Busby, west of Highway 212 in the Rosebud/Ree area and at an area called Muddy Cluster, about four miles from west of Lame Deer These areas are developing because of the increasing Cheyenne population

ASHLAND DISTRICT

Stubborn/Shy People (*Totoemana*)

The Cheyenne People from this district were distant from the other Cheyenne families who lived in other parts of the reservation They did not get involved with problems, and they were the last people to be involved in matters such as politics While some said they were "shy people," they were not bashful They stayed in their area minding their own business and helping each other The translation for Totoemana is difficult, Rev Rodolphe Petter gave the meaning as "Standoffish," and another meaning is "Unwilling Place " [3]

These families were more involved with the St. Labre Mission, and they would often camp nearby to be close to their children who were in school there. These families had their own gatherings, their own world. Someone would probably describe them like the Amish today. During the ration days, they were the last to come in for their rations. They lived quiet lives and only came out when something was happening. This is why their district was called Rabbit Town. Supposedly, rabbits stay within their homes and only come out when something is happening.[4]

Before 1900 when the reservation was enlarged to its current size, these families had settled east of the Tongue River. Since these lands were not included within the reservation boundaries, the families were not eligible to receive any assistance from the Tongue River Agency.

These families were starving and in an impoverished state. The St. Labre Mission dispensed medicine and offered whatever it could to them. After the second Executive Order changed the boundary to the middle of the Tongue River, James McLaughlin, special agent, settled with these families. For payment of $25 each, they left their home sites on the east side and settled along the west side of the Tongue River valley.[5]

Northern Cheyenne Indian Reservation

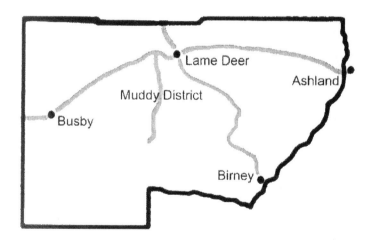

BIRNEY

There are really two Birneys For lack of a better descriptor, the one located about nine miles south of the reservation is called "White" Birney by the Cheyenne people This Birney was named after one of the troops who may have been a colonel in the U S cavalry The other Birney is located on the reservation and has a unique history all its own

Oevemanaheno Birney District
Scabby People Place

There was a man named *Oevemaha* who settled in this area The people who settled with him in this area were called *O'evemana* Oevemanaheno became the name of this place This word means barren—no trees, no vegetation with only cactus growing, much like they describe the place where peyote is found [6] Weist said that the Cheyennes near Birney were known as Scabbies because one of their leaders called Badger had some sort of skin rash However this was a poor translation, and the people from this district do not like this translation [7]

BUSBY DISTRICT

Vohpoometaneno

Busby was named after Sheridan L Busby, a farmer and rancher who originally owned 160 acres within the reservation Busby opened the first store, and eventually the community came to be named Busby Prior to the permanent establishment of the reservation, some white settlers had filed for their homesteads in this area, and these homesteaders were paid to move off the reservation by McLaughlin

WHITE RIVER

White River People (*Vohpoometaneo'o*)

In 1879 after the Little Wolf and Dull Knife bands had left Oklahoma Territory, the remaining Cheyenne families under Little Chief were transferred to the Pine Ridge Agency where they occupied the lands near White River in South Dakota These Cheyenne families were the last to arrive on the Northern Cheyenne Reservation When they were transferred to this agency in 1881, these families settled in the Busby area and called it the White River place [8]

LAME DEER DISTRICT

Mo'ohtavoheomeneno Black Lodge or *Meave'ho'eno* The Giving Place

The town of Lame Deer was named after Chief Lame Deer, a Minneconjou

Lakota who was killed in 1877 in a battle held south of Lame Deer. The creek that runs through the town of Lame Deer was named Antelope Creek by the Cheyenne, and it's possible that there is some correlation in translating the name to Lame Deer as well. White Bull saved Brigadier General Nelson A. Miles's life during the skirmish with the Lakota chief whose name is borne by the stream and the town.[9]

Miles had supported the Northern Cheyenne remaining in this area. In his letter dated June 1 1889, he stated, "There is no good reason or justice in removing the Indians from this area." In the winter of 1877, the Indians surrendered in good faith. The principal ones (Two Moons, White Bull, Horse Roads, Iron Shield, and Brave Wolf) were the first to come in and surrender and open the way for the surrender of the entire Lakota camp of Sitting Bull and Crazy Horse.

This group of Northern Cheyenne assisted General Miles's expedition against Lame Deer's band of 60 lodges. Chief Lame Deer, along with several principal warriors, was killed and captured. This expedition ended Indian hostilities in this territory. According to General Miles, "There is no reason why Indians cannot be well treated and allowed to live in peace in the vicinity in which they were born. They were told that if they remained at peace and did what they were directed to do, the Government would treat them fairly and justly. They have fulfilled their part of the compact and it would be but justice for the Government to allow them to remain."[10]

BLACK LODGE PEOPLE

Mo'ohtavoheomenetaneo'o

This name "Black Lodge People" was given to the families that lived in this area. It was a mean joke due to their lodges being blackened by smoke from burning pine. The joke is that the people were lazy, and they would not leave to go out and get cottonwood or ash wood to burn. Instead they burned pine, which caused their lodges to get all black from the pitch. The people stayed close to the Lame Deer agency because it was a ration point and they did not want to miss out on anything if they left the agency. The other districts used to get mad at them for getting everything, and this name stuck. The people living in Lame Deer were called Black Lodge People.[11] Because this was the place where rations were given out, the Cheyennes called the Giving Place, thus the second name, Meave'ho'eno, for Lame Deer, MT.

MUDDY CREEK (*HEOVONEHEO'HE'E*)

Heovoneheo'he'e tsehestahese (Those who are from Muddy Creek)

Muddy Creek got its name because there was hardly any water in this creek, and there were a lot of mud holes. The Cheyenne used to call this creek "Fat Horse Creek," and they wintered their horses in this area due to the salt sage that grew there. The horses got fat from eating this sage, and with their horses near by, the Cheyennes had the opportunity to hunt in the Wild Hog Basin. When Little Wolf went into self-exile after killing a Cheyenne the Elk Horn Scrappers went with him to this area. [12]

OTHER SIGNIFICANT RESERVATION AREAS

Ononeno Rosebud/Ree District

This is the area of Rosebud Creek between Busby and Muddy Creek. Stories that come down from our ancestors relate that the Cheyenne who migrated from Great Lakes area to eastern North Dakota once lived in villages near the Mandan and Arikara (Ree) Tribes. There was inter-marriage among the people, and these descendents settled in what the older people call the Ree District. [13] It is not considered an official district and, politically, is part of the Muddy Creek District.

Pono'e Downstream

Pono'e for those who live in Busby means the area from Busby to Muddy Creek, including the Rosebud-Ree area. For those who live in Lame Deer and Muddy, Pono'e means that area toward Jimtown and Jimtown itself.

He'ameo'he'e Upstream

For those people who live in the Busby area, He'ameo'he'e is that area upstream from Busby to the Kirby area. For those who live in Lame Deer and Muddy Creek areas, He'ameo'he'e is that area upstream toward Busby and Kirby.

1 Weist, T (1977) *A history of the Cheyenne people* (p 104) Billings Montana Council for Indian Education

2 McLaughlin, J (1899) *McLaughlin report on proposed removal of the Northern Cheyenne Indians and related matters* 55th Congress, House of Representatives, Document No 153

3 http //www geocities com/cheyenne_language/alphabet htm retrieved Dec 2007

4 B Rogers (personal communication)

5 McLaughlin (1899)

6 B Rogers (personal communication)

7 Weist, *A History of the Northern Cheyenne People,* pp 164 & 172

8 Weist *A History of the Northern Cheyenne People,* pp 161 & 172

9 Powell, P J , (1998) *Sweet Medicine The continuing role of the Sacred Arrow, the Sun Dance and the Sacred Buffalo Hat in Northern Cheyenne history* (Vol 1, p 6) Norman University of Oklahoma Press

10 McLaughlin 1899

11 L Tall Bull (personal communication)

12 L Tall Bull (personal communication)

13 A Spang (personal communication)

Agriculture on the Northern Cheyenne Reservation

THE NORTHERN CHEYENNE people have an agricultural past, rooted in their long migration from the Hudson's Bay and Great Lakes region westward This journey included several decades in the late 18th century spent living as farmers along the Missouri River Part of the Cheyenne legacy of farming has been unearthed in the Upper Midwest by archaeologists [2] People living in villages of earthen lodges grew squash, beans, and corn there prior to 1770

Another part of this legacy is remembered in ceremonialism, the Cheyenne Corn Dance or the Ree Ceremony, which survived to 1877, long after the Cheyennes left their earthen lodges and villages in the eastern Dakotas The ceremonies died out during the wars and turmoil of the period Anthropologist Robert Anderson quotes Nancy Divesbackwards in the 1950s as remarking, perhaps a little cynically, that "Indians were in the wars, and nobody paid attention to ceremonies "[3] The Corn Dance was a healing ceremony, but the planting of corn was also accompanied by a special corn planting dance, overseen by a Corn Master, and performed by couples while men sang and kept time with elk horn scrapers But the corn planting dance, too, disappeared as the Northern Cheyennes moved west of the Black Hills [4] Today, the memory of corn farming remains in the name Corn Woman, or Corn Tassel Woman, a common name on the reservation used even today

After the Northern Cheyennes acquired horses and began to pursue the buffalo in the late 1700s, the cultivation of farms was impractical Still, the harvesting of plants was important for a balanced diet, medicine, and ceremonial uses Always on the go, the Cheyennes necessarily developed a talent for identifying and using wild plants, adapting them to their use in a variety of ways [5] "There are no weeds on the reservation," the late tribal elder William Tall Bull used to say, as he and his son Linwood strived to keep the traditional Cheyenne knowledge of plants alive

In the late 19th century, when the Northern Cheyenne Reservation was created, the question of how the Cheyennes would make a living there became especially important. At first glance, the rugged pine-covered hills of the reservation seemed unsuitable to farming, yet, as James McLaughlin, then an inspector for the Indian Bureau, pointed out in 1899, "the Northern Cheyenne Reserve is probably the best cattle range in the state of Montana."[6]

Congress appropriated $60,000 for a shipment of a thousand heifers and bulls in 1902 and 1907. Since the government's policy emphasized individual ownership of resources, cattle were branded "ID" (Indian Department) on one side and the number of the individual owner on the other. Nevertheless, the cattle ranged through the reservation as a kind of single herd and were left to fend for themselves in the winter. The operation was overseen by a non-Indian employee of the agency, who hired both Indian and non-Indian cowboys to assist with the roundups. For the next few years, the cattle business on the Northern Cheyenne Reservation proved highly successful, with as many as 12,000 head fetching high prices in the Chicago market.[7]

Cheyenne cowboys are pictured about 1910 near Lame Deer in the annual ritual of branding. Left to right: Louie Seminole, Highwalker, and Wild Hog (standing). (Photo from the Mennonite collection)

Cheyenne cowboys were not identified in this picture, which is believed to have been taken in about 1910 near Lame Deer. (Photo from the Mennonite collection)

One of the obstacles to the cattle business on the reservation was the frequent occurrence of cattle killing. The 1890s were one of the most desperate periods in Northern Cheyenne history. Cheyennes sometimes slaughtered cattle for food when no other food was available. When these slaughtered cattle belonged to white ranchers, tensions between the Cheyennes and their white neighbors rose significantly, especially since these ranchers had fought hard to keep the federal government from establishing a reservation for the Northern Cheyennes along the Rosebud and Tongue Rivers.

The Head Chief and Young Mule incident of 1890 and the No Brains and Walks Night conflict a year later demonstrate the serious repercussions of cattle killing. Head Chief was a young man who had never had a chance to prove himself in battle. With a teenaged friend John Young Mule, he killed a cow belonging to a neighboring rancher. When the rancher's nephew, Hugh Boyle, caught the two butchering the meat, Head Chief shot him and hid the body. Nevertheless, Boyle's body was found, and the authorities threatened the Cheyennes with arrest unless the murderer was found. Head Chief told Chief American Horse to tell the soldiers and Indian police that he would come into the agency on Friday— ration day— but to be prepared: He was prepared to die like a man.

On the chosen day, Head Chief and Young Mule appeared at the top of a ridge to the northeast of the present location of Chief Dull Knife College. In an act of suicidal bravery, the two youths rode headlong into a line of Indian police, who shot them down at the bottom of the hill,[8] while the chiefs rode back and forth in front of a group of young Cheyennes to make sure that none would try to interfere with the police and spark more violence [9]

The next year, two more Cheyennes, No Brains and Walks Night, again slaughtered a cow off the reservation and made a threat against the reservation agent to kill him Although No Brains was later caught and sent briefly to Fort Keogh, the threat resulted in the Army establishing Camp Merritt on the reservation in the event of trouble in the future [10]

The Head Chief and No Brains incidents demonstrate that the Cheyennes were hungry, not that they were lawless The rations promised by the government were not provided in sufficient supply to feed the people They teach us about the violence that poverty and hunger can do to a community

RANCHING V FARMING

Sporadic cattle killing continued for the first two decades of the 20th century, often resulting from some tribal members' deep-seated resentment of white ranchers leasing their lands John R Eddy was superintendent of the Tongue River Reservation from 1906 to 1914 [11] He was an idealist and dreamer Backed by his close friend George Bird Grinnell, Eddy envisioned a reservation fully stocked with Cheyenne cattle, but until that objective could be met, he would sell grazing permits for the Cheyenne range to white ranchers

To increase the number of Indian cattle, he and Grinnell proposed to the Indian Bureau an elaborate plan for Congress to make additional appropriations To manage the herd and curtail cattle killing, Eddy and Grinnell proposed to convert the fences on the reservation to telephone wires and send the Indian police along the reservation perimeter ready to call in any infractions, just as Grinnell noted policemen did in New York City [12]

In addition, Eddy envisioned a young men's association designed to turn young Cheyennes away from cattle killing and toward a career in stock raising It probably is no accident that Eddy's idea coincided with the rise nationally of the original Boys Clubs of America, and Eddy's proposal included a clubhouse with a circulating library, and even a football team Eddy's superiors sharply disagreed with further Congressional appropriations for the herd or Eddy's management proposals, with the result that Eddy and Grinnell never saw their dreams fulfilled [13]

Farming was part of Eddy's plan for reservation development, and although it took second place to cattle raising, it nonetheless resulted in one of the largest collective work projects in the history of the reservation The southern portion of the reservation, with Tongue River on its east, seemed adaptable to farming if irrigation could be developed

In 1907, the Tongue River Irrigation Project, commonly called the Birney Ditch, was begun. Bad luck plagued the project almost from the beginning. Three successive floods in the first year of construction washed away much of the progress. A very low water level in the canal, alkali seepage, and land slides all contributed to a final cost of $300 per acre, which was unacceptable to the policymakers of the time. [14]

Eddy, for all of his idealism, was a remarkably poor manager, and in 1914 he was replaced by John Buntin, whose administration emphasized dry-land farming. Thus the Birney Ditch fell into disrepair and was abandoned by 1918.

The years of construction on the Birney Ditch coincided with other construction projects on the reservation, as well as the construction of railroads along and to the north of the Yellowstone River. During this period, "any Cheyenne desiring wage work could find it on this project," according to Robert Pringle, who studied the reservation in the 1950s.[15] The availability of jobs for the Northern Cheyennes meant a marked decrease in cattle killing and other related problems. But after the Birney Ditch, the Milwaukee Road Railroad, and other projects were completed in 1912, the cattle killing spiked, indicating that when work disappears, other means of survival will certainly be found.

Cattle and branding are still an important part of life on the Northern Cheyenne Reservation in the 21st century. From left to right are Vernon Small; Jason Lawrence; Clinton Small, Sr. (branding); Rowdy Alexander; Allen Fisher (on the horse); Kermit Spang; and Merlin Killsnight. (Photo by John Warner)

Superintendent John Buntin's emphasis on farming was part of a larger, bureau-wide focus on the development of individual family farms [16] Buntin, a relatively benevolent but often heavy-handed administrator, was eager for Northern Cheyenne farmers to show off their produce, especially in local and statewide agricultural fairs, as indicated by this circular to farmers in 1918

> You are hereby directed to gather the best exhibits of all the different crops of the reservation and have them in readiness for exhibit as it has been in the past Do not neglect to gather and prepare your exhibits at the appointed time You can select very good exhibits by taking them as you are going around in connection with your other work Urge every Indian, who has something creditable, to save a portion for display This is in compliance with the Indian Office wishes and you are requested to give it your special attention [17]

Northern Cheyenne families seemed amenable to Buntin's program, especially during the World War I years when wheat fetched a premium at the market By 1918, sales of farm produce exceeded those of livestock, and by 1920, an actual manpower shortage existed at harvest time [18] Yet both agricultural projects— farming and stock raising— were doomed to failure by the continuing federal emphasis on individual ownership and production Buntin and his successors distributed the tribal herd to individual families, giving owners more flexibility to sell, with the result that the number of Cheyenne cattle dropped from 7,000 in 1920 to under 3,000 in 1932 [19]

Similar pressure to divide the reservation into individual allotments made it increasingly difficult for Cheyennes to live off the land The federal policy from the late 19th century until 1934 was to divide reservations into allotments for individual Indians who were deemed competent and to open the "surplus" to homesteading by non-Indians [20] On the Northern Cheyenne Reservation, the bureau made all the allotments in the arid rangeland, not in the pine-forested hills, which could have provided a few Cheyennes with a reasonable living selling timber As the drought of the 1920s grew increasingly dire, it was clear that a 160-acre allotment would not provide enough land for Cheyenne farmers to raise the kind of crops needed to provide for their families [21]

Clearly the most effective agricultural use of the Northern Cheyenne Reservation was for cattle, as McLaughlin had observed in 1899 In 1937, the tribal council launched the Northern Cheyenne Steer Enterprise, which enjoyed considerable success in its early years The tribe purchased steers from the warmer Southwest, fattened them on the reservation range, and then sold them at market The system was so successful that it was copied during the World War II years by one of Montana's largest stockmen Matt Tschergi, who controlled vast ranges on the neighboring Crow Reservation [22]

The Steer Enterprise functioned a little like the Tennessee Valley Authority in that it provided opportunities to the community that went far beyond simply raising steers Cheyenne farmers were able to sell hay and other supplies to the enterprise, they could lease pastures to it, they could even sell calves to the business [23]

Eventually, though, the Steer Enterprise declined and disappeared Cheyenne ranchers clamored for the business to buy their stock instead of steers purchased in the Southwest An unusually harsh winter in 1949 took its toll on the herd The profits were disbursed in three per capita payouts, rather than being invested in new stock By 1958, the Steer Enterprise had ended [24]

THE NEW DEAL

The 1930s also brought the New Deal to the Northern Cheyenne Reservation Just as the Civilian Conservation Corps (CCC) provided work for thousands of unemployed Americans during the Great Depression, the Indian CCC provided good jobs to men living on reservations, including the Northern Cheyenne Historians have often mentioned that the Depression was less of a jolt to Indian reservations, since they had always existed in a state of economic depression and joblessness If anything, the New Deal brought opportunities to reservations that many Indian people had never seen before

At first, Cheyennes were wary of signing up for the Indian CCC, believing it to be a ploy by the government to conscript them to fight in overseas wars Yet by fall of 1933, over 200 Cheyennes had signed up to work in five camps on the reservation The supervisor of work relief programs on the reservation even reported that "fully 90% of able-bodied men at Tongue River Reservation and all Indian unemployment is absorbed "[25] Elder Ted Risingsun remembers that before the Indian New Deal programs, Cheyenne men were often employed by off-reservation ranches as line riders but the Indian CCC provided enough jobs that off-reservation work was no longer necessary

Among their many projects, the workers for the Tongue River Indian CCC eradicated prairie dog towns and poisonous plants like larkspur, built hundreds of miles of fences, and even repaired and restored the Birney Ditch And, like CCC camps across the nation, the Cheyenne camps provided movies and sports programs By the beginning of World War II, the Cheyenne workers had significantly increased the value of their range by building corrals, wells, and 240 miles of trails for fire trucks [26] The Indian CCC proved immensely popular with Cheyenne farmers, whose drought-stricken homesteads had left them with little hope for the future Yet other Cheyennes sometimes criticized them Anthropologist Robert Anderson, for instance, recorded several tribal members (Pius Shoulderblade, Henry Standing Elk, and Milton Whiteman) implying that the government programs of the 1930s effectively killed farming on individual allotments [27] Yet the programs began just at the moment when drought and wheat prices were at their worst The choice to forsake the family farm for wage labor was a rational one and one that was made by American farmers nationwide

Since the ending of the Indian CCC and the Steer Enterprise, agriculture continued to be an important part of the reservation economy, although the Bureau of the Census in 2002 reported only about 50 Indian-owned farms and ranches (out of a total of 64) on a reservation that is home to a little over 4,000 people [28] A water compact negotiated with the state of Montana in 1991 eased credit worries among Cheyenne ranchers, some of whom had become modestly prosperous Many Northern Cheyenne people who are not actively engaged in ranching nevertheless owned various livestock, especially horses, and some cultivated family gardens

The story of Northern Cheyenne agriculture is really a lesson about economic development Tribal politics can be ferocious at times, leaving a few Cheyennes with a certain cynicism about the tribal government Yet in an impoverished community looking for ways for its people to find gainful employment, collective projects— as opposed to the individual emphasis of former government policies— have always done reasonably well in this community Examples include the Birney Ditch and other construction projects of the early 20th century, the first tribal cattle herd, the Indian Civilian Conservation Corps of the 1930s, and the Northern Cheyenne Steer Enterprise

In more recent years, the federally-sponsored Community Education and Training Act provided many Cheyennes with opportunities working in the public sector, and the reconstruction of the Tongue River Dam employed tribal members The success of these collective projects reflects, in a way, the success of the collective agriculture practiced by the Cheyennes in what is now North Dakota over 200 years ago Perhaps that memory, and the continuing commitment of many Cheyennes to work with Mother Earth rather than against her, explain what is and isn't successful on the Northern Cheyenne Reservation

1 Grinnell, G B (1962) *The Cheyenne Indians Their history and ways of life* (Vol 1, 4) New York Cooper Square Publishers

2 Wood, W R (1971) *Biesterfeldt A post-contact coalescent site on the north-eastern plains* Washington, DC Smithsonian Institution Press Kurtz, W M (1989) Early Cheyenne migrations and cultural change *South Dakota Archaeology 13*, 69-88

3 Anderson, R (1958) Notes on Northern Cheyenne corn ceremonialism *Masterkey for Indian Lore and History 32*(1), 62

4 Ibid

5 Hart, J (1981) The ethnobotany of the Northern Cheyenne Indians of Montana *Journal of Ethnopharmacology 4*(1)

6 Proposed removal of the Northern Cheyenne Indians, *House Document* 55th Cong, 3rd Session, no 153 (17 Jan 1899), 6

7 Anderson, R (1951) A study of Cheyenne culture history, with special reference to the Northern Cheyenne Doctoral dissertation, 186 (Ann Arbor, MI University of Michigan)

8 West, T (1984) *A history of the Northern Cheyenne People* (pp 136-137) Billings Montana Council for Indian Education

9 T Risingsun (personal communication), 1987

10 Weist, *A History of the Northern Cheyenne People*, p 137

11 The name of the reservation was officially changed from Tongue River to Northern Cheyenne when the reservation was expanded by Executive Order in 1900 However, the old name was still used until 1946, when the Bureau of Indian Affairs announced that "reference to these Indians as the Tongue River Indians or by any other name is entirely unwarranted and should be discontinued to avoid any confusion " Bureau of Indian Affairs, District No 2, Memorandum, Billings MT, 19 September 1946 National Archives and Research Administration (Denver), 8 NS 075 97 013, Box 15

12 Pringle, R M (1958) *The Northern Cheyenne Indians in the reservation period* Bachelor's of Arts thesis, 41 Cambridge Mass Harvard Pringle's honors thesis at Harvard remains one of the most useful sources for 20th century Northern Cheyenne history

13 Ibid , 41-42

14 Weist, *A History of the Northern Cheyenne People* p 163-164

15 Pringle, *The Northern Cheyenne Indians in the reservation period* 48

16 J Buntin to the Commissioner of Indian Affairs, 17 August 1917 Tongue River Agency, Lame Deer, MT National Archives and Research Administration (Denver) 8 NS 075 97 010, Box 28

17 Buntin J Circular to farmers, 28 July 1918 Tongue River Agency, Lame Deer, MT National Archives and Research Administration (Denver), 8 NS 075 97 010 Box 28

18 Pringle, *The Northern Cheyenne Indians in the reservation period* 57-58

19 Ibid , 61

20 Washburn, W W (1975) *The assault on Indian tribalism The General Allotment Law (Dawes Act) of 1887* (Philadelphia Lippincott)

21 Ibid , 63-64

22 See Randolph, E (1981) *Beef leather and grass* (Norman University of Oklahoma Press)

23 Weist, *A History of the Cheyenne People*, p 194

24 Pringle, *The Northern Cheyenne Indians in the reservation period*, 88

25 Ibid 71

26 Ibid , 75-78

27 Anderson, A study of Cheyenne culture history, 192-193

28 Cf <<http //www nass usda gov/mt/county/profiles/reservations/nchevenne htm>>

(Editor's note Plants can be poisonous Readers are advised not to eat plants or make tea from them without being absolutely sure of the identification Use in moderation)

THERE ARE MANY plants that were used by the American Indian people, and many still are It is important to understand that the Indian people have a very close relationship with all living things Everything has life Even the rocks have life, and of all things "Only the Rocks Live Forever "

TEAS

The tea plants used by the Cheyenne are mint, June berry, and rose bush The Cheyenne word for tea is *vehpotsehohpe* (flower or leaf soup) These teas are for everyday use, and as with many plants, they bring good memories, which contribute to the healing process

WILD MINT

This plant grows along the banks of streams, springs, and ponds and should be harvested before its blossoms turn to seeds All of the plants from the mint family can be identified not only by their smell but by the square stems

How to pick The good way to pick plants is to use a cutter of some sort so you can leave the roots This enables the plant to grow the following year Take your mint home, wash the plants with cold water, and tie the stems together Before you take them in the house, shake the water from them Find a good place to hang them to dry, never hang them in the sun to dry as they turn black and are not useable The mint gives your house a good smell as they are drying After they are completely dry, put them in a plastic bag for storage for future use Cheyennes would pick enough to last them through the winter

How to make tea Put a pot of water on the stove and place a handful of leaves and stems into the water When the water starts to boil, turn the stove off and let the tea steep for several minutes Cheyenne people would sweeten their tea with honey or sap from the box elder tree, which is a member of the sugar maple family

Use as a medicine: The mint tea is used for headaches and nausea Persons that suffer from depression should use this tea One of the important parts of healing this condition is to use the senses we are each born with (smell, taste, sight, feel, and hearing)

Cheyenne Name: *moxešene*
Botanical Name *Mentha arvensis*

Rose Bush

The rose hips were picked and eaten in the winter and were a good source of vitamin C The Cheyenne selected long stalks of rose bushes and using a knife, trimmed all the stickers and bark off a section and cut enough for a pot of tea The roots of the rose bush could be dug up and used for tea also The rose bushes grow along streams and ponds and are readily available The rose bush tea was the most popular for the hunters and war parties because of its availability

How to cook: The roots or peeled stalks are cut into small pieces and put in a vessel filled with water and boiled for several minutes and then allowed to steep for a minute or two The tea is pink in color and can be used to stop diarrhea A rose bush root that has been cut into one-inch pieces can be carried with you and used over and over for making the tea, the roots have a black outer shell

Cheyenne Name: *henenóe*
Botanical Name: *Rosa arkansasa*

June Berry / Sarvisberry

June berry bushes grow along streams and tributaries The bark can be used in the winter, and the leaves can be used in the summer Some Cheyenne used the large branches to construct ceremonial sweat lodges The protocol has been forgotten, and this wood is no longer used The berries ripen in early July and are eaten fresh or dried for future use The Cheyenne treasured the berry picking seasons as it was a time when families and various tribal bands gathered to pick the berries Many stories were told and feasts held It was a time of plenty with the abundance of wild game

How to cook: The green leaves or bark was stripped from branches and put in a vessel of water, which was heated When the water boiled, it was taken from the fire and allowed to steep for a couple of minutes A handful of leaves is the usual amount needed for brewing tea More water can be added to strong tea, but nothing can be done with weak tea My father (William Tall Bull) used to say, "It was so weak that it came to the table on crutches "

Cheyenne Name: *hetanemenotse*
Botanical Name: *Amelanchier alnifolia*

Berry Plants

Buffalo Berry

The Cheyenne word for berries is *menotse* The buffalo berry is a small berry and is usually red in color, but there are some bushes that produce yellow fruit The fruit is tart and very hard to pick Some people place a hide or canvas under the bush and knock the berries off with a stick This form of harvesting the berry is very damaging to the bushes and should not be encouraged My grandmother hand picked all her berries and used to comment that only lazy people used sticks The berries were dried on a hide or canvas and put into containers for future use

The buffalo berry is very useful as a pudding when a healer is doctoring a patient After the smudging and prayers the patient is offered food, and the first given is the tart pudding The experience of a hospital stay is a very frightening to the Cheyenne elders, and most feel that they will not return home The majority of the people that spend long periods in a hospital will give up and slowly starve themselves—they have no appetite However, the tartness of the buffalo berry pudding triggers the saliva glands and brings back the appetite, and then you can feed them the rest of the meal

How to cook. Place a handful of dried berries in a pot half filled with water, and let the berries boil until soft Next mix one cup of flour and two cups of water to make a thick mixture Pour this mixture into the boiling berries until you get the thickness that you want After the pudding is the desired consistency, then add sugar to your taste The dried buffalo berries can also be pounded up with dried meat to make pemmican This was a staple for the women that gathered wood and the hunters and warriors away from their villages Before wheat flour was introduced to the Cheyenne, the breadroot was used to thicken soups and puddings

Cheyenne Name: *ma'kemenotse / ma'kestatsemenotse*
Botanical Name: *Shepherdia canadensis*

Chokecherry

The chokecherry is probably the most popular of all berries Unlike other berries, it is hardy and grows every year The Cheyenne hunters would not shoot female animals (deer, elk, antelope, buffalo, and horses) until the chokecherries turned red. This was the time when the animals' young could survive on their own. As the berry ripens in July, it can be eaten fresh and the seed spit out, but usually the berry was picked and the stems taken off. The berries and pits were pounded on a pounding stone. The pounded berries were then made into patties and put on a hide and allowed to dry, at which time they could be stored for the winter. The pounded-up cherries constituted one of the basic ingredients for pemmican.

The chokecherry tree was used to make tipi stakes and pins, bows and arrow shafts, spears and coup sticks, root diggers, and other useful items for the families. Makeshift shelters of chokecherry limbs were used to make structures resembling the sweat lodge. These were used by warriors in the field, usually in the winter. The Cheyenne and Sioux constructed these dome-shaped lodges in the winter of 1866 for the warriors who were given instruction to harass the wood trains and the soldiers of Buffalo Creek Fort (Fort Phil Kearny).

How to cook: The dried chokecherries (about a handful) were put in a pot and boiled for several minutes, and a flour and water mixture was added to thicken the pudding. The sweeteners that the Cheyenne used were honey or sap from the box elder tree (maple family).

Cheyenne Name: *menótse*

Botanical Name: *Prunus virginiana*

Linwood Tall Bull follows in the footsteps of his father, William Tall Bull, and teaches ethnobotany at Chief Dull Knife College. (Photo by Sherry Ann Foote)

The Girl Who Saved Her Brother

MOST BATTLES WERE fought by men, but occasionally there were extremely brave women who went to war This was the case of Buffalo Calf Road Woman who saved her brother from death When the Cheyenne heard that General George Crook was leading a war party against them, the Cheyenne warriors rode out to halt the troops Several hundred Cheyenne and Sioux warriors attacked Crook and his soldiers near Rosebud Creek between present-day Sheridan, WY and Busby, MT, on June 17, 1876 She rode beside her husband, Black Coyote, and her brother, Chief Comes in Sight

During the battle Buffalo Calf Road Woman lost sight of her brother When she finally spotted him, he was surrounded by Crow Indian scouts and white soldiers waiting for a chance to count coup on him Chief Comes in Sight fought fiercely with great skill, but his horse was shot and killed during the fight leaving him vulnerable to the circling soldiers and scouts Buffalo Calf Road Woman charged the crowd of hostiles, dodging bullets, and grabbed her brother, carrying him to safety on her horse This brave rescue on her part caused the Cheyenne to rally and to defeat General Crook and his soldiers The Cheyenne refer to the battle as The Fight Where the Girl Saved Her Brother In history the battle is recorded as The Battle of the Rosebud

At the time of the battle Buffalo Calf Road Woman was in her mid twenties with one child, a girl about four years old Buffalo Calf Road Woman was the only woman to accompany the warriors and to fight in the battle There were two Crow women that fought as scouts for General Crook's army

One week later, the Battle of the Little Big Horn was fought, and Buffalo Calf Road Woman was the only woman to fight in the battle against Custer [1] She proved to be so brave and courageous the Cheyenne gave her an honorary name, Brave Woman The Battle of the Little Big Horn is one of the most written about events in American history, yet few know about her participation in this battle

Despite her many heroic efforts to defend the freedom and nomadic life style of her people, Buffalo Calf Road Woman has been overlooked in history Much of her history was never recorded[2] A nomadic life style and lack of a written language account for some of the absence of sources The narratives, letters, diaries, and other bits of information that exist are largely from the perspective of white interpreters

Male anthropologists, who dominated the field in the late 19th and early 20th century, rarely interviewed women and demonstrated little interest in women beyond their traditional roles Historians and anthropologists were mainly interested in chiefs, battles, and Indian-white politics

Photographers such as L A Huffman provided an important source of information about the Northern Cheyenne and other tribes However, they usually portrayed women engaging in domestic duties and rarely identified them Northern Cheyenne women were photographed many times with their husbands Captions would often read, for example, "Dull Knife and wife" or "Cheyenne woman "

Woodenlegs, a warrior who knew Buffalo Calf Road Woman and fought in the same battles, notes her role in the Battle of the Rosebud and relates the birth of her second child Unfortunately, he omits her significant participation at the Battle of the Little Big Horn There are only a few statements made by Northern Cheyennes connecting her to these two battles Chief Two Moons, who fought in both battles with Buffalo Calf Road Woman, failed to mention her in interviews White Bull and Tall Bull, Northern Cheyenne warriors, also did not acknowledge her noteworthy participation in battles[3] With the exception of Woodenleg's brief statement about her role in the Rosebud Battle, the Northern Cheyenne men were completely silent about her accomplishments

However, two Cheyenne women—Lion Teeth and Kate Bighead—attended many of the same events as Buffalo Calf Road Woman In their autobiographical accounts, the women give detailed narrative of her participation in the two battles A Sioux warrior, Kill Eagle, also credits and confirms Buffalo Calf Road Woman's presence at the Custer fight Kill Eagle reported seeing Buffalo Calf Road Woman with a revolver strapped on her, but he erroneously stated that she was killed[4]

In actuality, she lived and took an active role in the tribe's exodus to Oklahoma and subsequent escape During the cold winter of 1877, the Cheyenne were starving, and some women and children were being held hostage by the U S Army in an attempt to get them all to move to Indian Territory (Oklahoma) When most of the others decided to surrender, Buffalo Calf Road Woman and her husband, Black Coyote, continued to refuse The couple was among a small group of 34 Cheyenne who resisted the move to a reservation in Oklahoma During this period, Buffalo Calf Road Woman gave birth to her second child, a son Within

Bullets soar by Buffalo Calf Road Woman as she rescues her brother, Chief Comes In Sight, from a certain death. Buffalo Calf Road Woman dressed for battle with her finest elk tooth dress, a broad leather belt, and a decorative choker around her neck. Chief Comes In Sight, who is wearing a long-tailed war bonnet, has his right arm and leg draped over the horse's neck with his left hand holding the rein. This horse is a fast one, indicated by the split ears. (Drawing from the Spotted Wolf-Yellow Nose Ledger, courtesy of the Smithsonian Institution, National Anthropological Archives, Bureau of American Ethnology, ms. 166.032)

the group there were several children, and there was so much suffering, the small band decided to surrender. In August 1877 the group reached Oklahoma.

Life in the Indian Territory proved very difficult for the Cheyenne. Hunting rights were denied, and diseases such as measles and malaria spread among the people. Unaccustomed to the humid climate and living with restrictions, the Cheyennes longed for their homeland. When 300 Cheyenne left Indian Territory, Buffalo Calf Road Woman and her family were among them. The journey back to Montana was 1,500 miles.

The Army followed and attacked them the whole way. Many grew weak with the constant threat from the soldiers. With the soldiers on their trail some wanted to surrender, but Black Coyote had not lost his fighting spirit and encouraged the people to persevere. Little Wolf and Dull Knife decided to split the group. Some wanted to return to Red Cloud's reservation. Black Coyote and Buffalo Calf Road Woman followed Little Wolf's party to return to the north. Black Coyote, Buffalo Calf Road Woman, and others held out and hid in the Sand Hills of Nebraska for the winter.

Meanwhile, Black Coyote grew more militant against the Army. He committed some acts that compromised the safety of the small band. Unrest and hostility among the group broke out, and Black Coyote killed a fellow Cheyenne and wounded another Chief Little Wolf ordered the exile of Black Coyote for these crimes Buffalo Calf Road Woman, Black Coyote, their children and four others left the main group The banished group remained hidden in the Sand Hills of Nebraska where there was plenty of game and few white people Later that spring, Black Coyote killed a soldier, and the group was captured and imprisoned at Fort Keogh Buffalo Calf Road Woman contracted diphtheria and died in captivity in 1879 Black Coyote was so distraught when he heard of Buffalo Calf Road Woman's death, he took his own life [5]

American Indian women are extraordinary and have survived unspoken hardships Information sources are limited, vague, and biased The most reliable and thorough historical records concerning American Indian women have proven to be other Native women Buffalo Calf Road Woman may have been forgotten if Iron Teeth and Kate Bighead had not conveyed the important acts of this distinguished woman

1 Grinnell, G B (1972) *Cheyenne Indians, Vol 2 War, ceremonies, and religion* Lincoln University of Nebraska Press

2 Agonito, R , & Agonito, J (1981) Resurrecting history's forgotten women A case study from the Cheyenne Indians *Frontiers A Journal of Women Studies 6* (3), 8-16

3 Agonito & Agonito (1981)

4 Graham W (1953) *The Custer Myth a source book of Custeriana* Harrisburg PA Stackpole Company

5 Agonito & Agonito (1981)

Cheyenne Peace Pipe

A STORY BY JOHN Stands in Timber tells that the first pipes the Cheyenne made were of antelope shanks, just the straight hollow bone, with a hole drilled on top at one end and the place wrapped and tied with sinew to keep it from splitting When the Cheyenne first got the red stone, they made it into a pipe in the same way, straight and hollow and it was good for this purpose

There were four old pipes made this way by the early people, and there used to be one large one pipe and three smaller pipes that were be kept in the Sacred Hat In fact all Indian pipes used to be made straight that way, until the white man came along with a corncob pipe sticking up That is how they came to make peace pipes the way they do now "[1]

In the Cheyenne culture, smoking the pipe is a solemn occasion and only done after prayer The Cheyenne say, "The pipe never fails" Nothing sacred begins without first offering the pipe to the Sacred Persons who dwell at the four directions, to *Ma'heo'o* and to Grandmother Earth When smoking the pipe, only the truth is spoken and nothing but the truth [2]

Stories have been told that in March 1869 Custer had met with Chief Medicine Arrow's band under along the Sweetwater Creek This was after the Attack on Washita Nov 27, 1868 There were two white women captives at this camp, and Custer did not want to attack the Cheyenne for fear of death to the captives Custer in a peaceful meeting smoked the ceremonial peace pipe with Chief Medicine Arrow At the conclusion of the meeting, Chief Medicine Arrow emptied the ashes of the pipe on Custer's boot in a gesture of future bad luck If he lied to the Cheyenne, he would become like those ashes Custer went against his word, and he was killed at the Battle of Little Big Horn in 1876 [3]

In photographs of the chiefs' visit to the Great White Father in Washington, DC, they are shown with their pipes in elaborate beaded pipe bags. Smoking the pipe signifies that a person is of good heart and being truthful

For Northern Cheyenne people like Chief Dull Knife, smoking a peace pipe signifies that a person is of good heart and being truthful.

1 Stands In Timber, J., & Liberty, M. (1967). *Cheyenne Memories* (p. 81). New Haven, CT: Yale University Press.

2 Powell, P. J. (1969). *Sweet Medicine: The Continuing Role of the Sacred Arrows, the Sun Dance, and the Sacred Buffalo Hat in Northern Cheyenne History.* Norman: University of Oklahoma Press. Vol. 1.

3 Greene, J. A. (2004). *Washita, the Southern Cheyenne and the U.S. Army.* Norman: University of Oklahoma Press.

Joseph Whitewolf Sr.

JOSEPH WHITEWOLF SR., a member of the Northern Cheyenne Tribe, was a Prisoner of War during World War II. The Germans captured him in central Europe, and he spent nine months as a prisoner. PFC Whitewolf was held in many different cities in Germany, according to the family.

On Dec. 25, 1944, he was sent to a work camp in what was then Czechoslovakia and stayed there until he was released in 1945. As a prisoner, PFC Whitewolf suffered greatly. He lost 50 pounds because of being fed only black bread and water, and he was beaten with a bayonet. When freed, he had to be hospitalized for a month to recover from his mistreatment.

In 1993, Whitewolf's family was presented with a POW Medal for honorably serving his country as a Prisoner of War. The Veteran's Upward Bound program at Chief Dull Knife College helped the family with the application process. The medal was long overdue because PFC Whitewolf had died by the time he received this medal.

Joseph Whitewolf Sr.

Balloon Bomb in Lame Deer

URING WORLD WAR II the Japanese were well acquainted with the pre-vailing winds that blow from Japan towards North America. The air flows eastward across the United States and Canada. In lower regions the winds are variable and often stormy. If the winds are high above the storms, a current of air called the jet stream flows across the earth at speeds of 300 miles per hour. [1]

Japanese used the jet steam to launch balloons carrying bombs. The balloons traveled 6,000 miles across the ocean. The concept of launching bomb-carrying balloons was a sophisticated and economical tactic. Utilizing the natural air forces took careful long-range planning and an understanding of nature. The Japanese called the balloons the Wind Ship Weapon and hoped they would cause considerable destruction and panic on American soil.

The Wind Ship Weapon campaign began in 1944. Japanese propaganda claimed that widespread fires and 500 casualties were a result of the balloons. The Japanese anticipated that the United States would withdraw troops from the South Pacific to protect the homeland. American and Canadian media were told to keep the balloon attacks unpublished. The U.S. Office of War issued a silence order, not wanting to give the impression that the balloon launching was successful. During 1944 there may have been 300 balloon bomb incidents throughout the United States but the media respected the order to be silent.

In January 1945, a balloon bomb landed near Lame Deer, MT. The incident occurred about 15 miles outside of Lame Deer up Muddy Creek. Juanita Lone Bear was just seven years old when she and her brother James and a group of neighbor children spotted the balloon floating through the sky.

Juanita was in the first grade at the local one-room school. There were six students, ranging in age from first to seventh grade, and Juanita was the youngest. Normally, she and her brother rode on horse back to school, but this cold Janu-

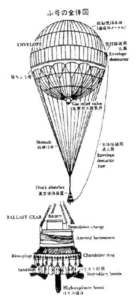

ふ号の全体図

ENVELOPE

Gas relief valve

Shrouds

Envelope destructor fuse

Shock absorber

BALLAST GEAR   Battery
Demolition charge
Aneroid barometers
Blow-plug   Chandelier ring
Sandbags   Incendiary bombs
High-explosive bomb

The Type A Paper Balloon

At the Lame Deer site, the balloon, 19 shrouds, and the gas relief valve were recovered. Constructed of panels of laminated tissue paper, the balloons were a well disguised weapon. (Illustration from the book, *Silent Siege*)

ary morning they walked to school instead. The Rowland children accompanied Juanita and James on the long walk home. The group took a two-mile cut across to shorten the six-mile trek home.

Franklin Rowland, a friend of Juanita's and James, saw the balloon and thought the moon was falling. Franklin kept pointing to the sky and saying, "The moon is falling." The balloon was grazing the tops of the trees, and some apparatus was dangling by a rope. The big ball barely cleared the hill and was rapidly descending. The children were alarmed, thinking the moon really might have fallen.

The children ran home to report the incident to their parents. The Rowlands went out that evening on horseback to look for the object, but darkness ended the search. Juanita and her folks went out the next morning in the family pickup truck to search for the balloon. Juanita's mother spotted the balloon on a steep creek bank. The grayish colored tarp was about as wide as a road, Juanita said.

Sixty-seven years later, Juanita vividly remembers the image of the strange object and what a close call they had. She said: "At the bottom of the balloon was a small box that was connected to a rope There had been other ropes, but they had been cut off by hitting trees and dragging on the ground There was a torpedo-shaped object about 1 1/2 feet long We were curious and poked around the thing examining it We wondered what on earth it was " [2]

Her parents thought it should be reported and turned in to the agent in Lame Deer, which they did "The agent was interested in the location of the landing There was to be no publicity, we were told, so the Japanese would not know their bomb-launching balloon had landed on U S soil," she said

The Japanese balloons and their bombs were intended to self-destruct at the end of a cycle, however, many malfunctioned and were found somewhat intact much like the Lame Deer balloon It is believed the wet cell batteries froze, making the circuits inoperative

Thinking back, Juanita realized how lucky they were They had dragged it around, thrown it into the back of the truck, and traveled over gravel and dirt roads "It could have gone off at any time If my brother would have had his gun, he probably would have shot at it "

1 Webber, B (1992) *Silent Siege-III Japanese attacks on North America in World War II* Medford, OR Webb Research Group

2 Lone Bear, J (personal communication), Nov 15, 2007

At Sgt. Uriah Two Two's victory dance, the ceremonial smudges on his face, combined with his Army uniform, captivated photographer Gwendolen Cates (author of the photo book, *Indian Country*).

Uriah Two Two

L OOK IN THE dictionary under the word "noble," and you will find Sgt Uriah Two Two At least that is what Kathleen Beartusk tells people about her youngest son In 2007, Two Two was in Iraq for his third tour with the 101st Airborne Division Two Two enlisted in the Army in 1998 and in 2006, he re-enlisted until 2012

This troubled his mother "I am definitely not looking forward to another year of anxiety, worry, sleeplessness, and fear of watching the news ' However, she said, "I know deep down in my heart that he is doing exactly what he's wanted to do since he was 5 years old Uriah is the epitome of what a soldier should be "

Two Two received a hero's welcome at the Billings Logan International Airport when he returned home after his first tour in Iraq in March 2004 He earned a Purple Heart for wounds he received when a roadside bomb went off More than 150 people gathered

In a traditional Northern Cheyenne ceremony at the airport, Two Two was blessed and cleansed by smoke from burning sweetgrass fanned by eagle feathers A war bonnet was placed on Two Two, and he was wrapped in a red, white, and blue star quilt Women's high-pitched ululating pierced the air No one touched Two Two until the ceremony was conducted to remove the aftereffects of war, according to a report in the *Billings Gazette*

He and his wife, Alma, have four children Jacob, Cathryn, Bresais, and Uriah, Jr His mother, Kathleen Beartusk, has worked at Chief Dull Knife College (CDKC) for 26 years A graduate of Chief Dull Knife College, she has raised five children as a single mom The children are sixth generation descendants of Chief Dull Knife

(Reprinted with permission from *Tribal College Journal*, Vol 17, No 3, Winter 2006, www tribalcollegejournal org)

THE SUBJECT OF spirit people is difficult As we all know everyone of us has a spirit, and it will remain here long after we are gone Your spirit is going to be here, yours and mine Those who have gone on, their spirits remain The customs of each tribe differ a little But they all focus on what is going to happen to the spirit

I had an opportunity a couple of years ago to be on the lands of one who had been dead for many years They put them in a box to be studied They decided that perhaps they would put back and bury him [The skeleton had been found during road construction] I volunteered to do that, to bury him, because I did not want that poor man to be sitting in a box on a shelf somewhere Not only that, but somehow I had to make sure that his spirit was also there

I went to this office, and I saw him and I saw this box on a table Then I began talking to him I told him that he had lived 70 years with his people and that he was a great man, that when he was buried all his people that loved him came to see him for the last time, that many people would go there after he was buried to talk to his spirit I told him that I would, with respect, offer him smoke, and I told him that I would be honored to return him to this resting place I said you have now satisfied the curiosity of many people, and from this point we will go back I will take you back to be buried where you belong

I went back to the reservation I went to the countryside, and during the course of the reburial there was this spirit that came from the south The spirit of people when it comes back, it comes back form the south He came as a whirl-wind We watched him come down the valley, and then he went right on by as if to acknowledge the ritual

It is quite difficult to rebury a person because there are usually a few words that are spoken to him after he has passed on "Now that you have left, go You do not turn around and look back " We believe that if they look back, they may take a child with them We teach our little ones—do not visit the graves of our people in the evening If they do, those spirits may follow the kids home and they will have trouble sleeping at night All of you have a spirit

I don't think we understand the spirit world well enough We understand it, we have lived it We understand the spirit nature of earth, the plants, and the animal life The relationships between these spirits whether they are good or bad, they guarantee us spiritual well being If we bother them, it is not the thing that we want to do We tend to view that when we bury them We bury them once to put them away

I learned these things a long time ago when I was little My grandfather told me He said when I pass on, my spirit is not going to go where you people are going to go It's going to go where the spirits go And I will come to you in times I think this is why many people have a special regard for these mounds—they house the spirit world people Who are the others? Who are the ones who answer our prayers?

At the request of the State Preservation Office, I also buried a little girl found in the hills by children who had been playing in a cave They found the remains of a young child I was comfortable with that because that young girl was found by playing children And I believe she was happy that children did come there There was no problem with that Children are the spiritual nature of ourselves

When we talk to archaeologists, come five o'clock, that is when the archaeologist hangs up his boots, the day is over That is the time when our world, our spirit world, is beginning to wake up That's a time I would like to walk We have a river on the eastern edge of the reservation [the Tongue River] where they are going to build a railroad At some point one of these days, we are going to walk that probably with some archaeologists We're going to come to spirit along the wall who will stand for a moment and disappear I'll probably see it If this archaeologist isn't an Indian, he probably wouldn't see it As you look down the valley before the sun goes down, this is when the spirits come out We see many, many sorts of things that we understand are very significant and important to us But if no one else sees it, how are we going to convince anyone of the spirit life in the valley?

One of the reasons that the burial/ reburial is taught is that it depends upon who is being buried Some of these people are powerful people, and indeed they may be very fond of this spot, and so we have to deal with this in the reburial One of the things I have to rely on is that the final ceremony takes place with my elders They have to appear as one And they sing a song that goes with that It's just not something that you do everyday.

To bury that old man bothered me for a long time, I didn't know if I had done the right thing But I had sworn to take the box and return it to the grave I was willing to take whatever risk there was A lot of spirit things are not talked about. We have to talk until all the people understand that they are part of our lives.

When archaeologists surveyed the land, we had a lot of things that were very significant to our way of life such as plants. Plants are part of our life, ever since the beginning of the earth. The Creation stories include the spiritual, the sacred beginnings of the earth; everything that appeared on it was sacred. So, there was a sacred relationship between man, animals, and plant life and the earth from the very beginning. We still hold that and we strive to maintain spiritual harmony with the earth, plants, and animals.

(This paper is a transcription of a presentation by William Tall Bull at the First Joint Meeting of the Archaeological Society of Alberta and the Montana Archaeological Society, May 2-6, 1990, at Waterton Lakes National Park, Alberta, Canada. The papers were published in a book, Kunaitupii. The article is published here with permission from the Archaeological Society of Alberta.)

William Tall Bull

William Tall Bull was born at Muddy Creek on the Northern Cheyenne Indian Reservation. He attended the government boarding school at Busby, MT. He became interested in history listening to the stories of his grandparents, who survived the Sand Creek Massacre in Colorado in 1864 and the long trek to Oklahoma and back to Montana In September of 1942, he went into World War II and became a radio operator in the Army Air Force He served in the Army during the occupation after the war

Tall Bull spent much of his life on the Northern Cheyenne Reservation serving his tribe, including a position as a councilman for the Northern Cheyenne He became an assistant history professor at Chief Dull Knife College, teaching oral traditions and ethno-botany classes From 1983 through 1995, he served as chairman of the Northern Cheyenne Tribal Cultural Protection Board In 1990, he received the Montana State Historic Preservation Award, the first American Indian so honored by the state of Montana

Tall Bull was instrumental in the passage of the Native American Grave Protection and Repatriation Act, having worked with former U S Sen John Melcher of Montana on the initial draft of that legislation He was later appointed by former Secretary of the Interior Manual Lujan, Jr, to sit on the committee that wrote the regulations for this act Tall Bull was the only American Indian to serve on that committee He served as an at-large member of the Fort Phil Kearny/ Bozeman Trail Association

In his ongoing efforts to safeguard the American Indian culture and heritage, he was a founder of the Medicine Wheel Alliance, an organization committed to preserving the Medicine Wheel National Historic Landmark in the Bighorn Mountains

This commitment to landmark preservation led former President Clinton in 1994 to appoint Tall Bull to become the first American Indian ever to serve on the Advisory Council on Historic Preservation, a national panel committed to protecting historical landmarks across the country

He passed on March 7, 1996

Northern Cheyenne Sacred Sites and Objects

A s with all American Indian tribes, the Northern Cheyenne hold some sites and objects as very sacred and central to their spiritual and tribal well being Some of these are described below

BEAR BUTTE

This sacred mountain near Sturgis, SD, is known as *Noavose* to the Cheyenne, meaning "The Hill Where the People Are Taught " This mountain resembles a large grizzly bear and is the heart of the Cheyenne sacred places and sacred ways Sweet Medicine, a prophet of the Cheyenne people, received the Four Sacred Arrows from *Ma'heo'o* (All Father and supreme deity) at Noavose

Peter J Powell chronicled Sweet Medicine and the Cheyenne people in a two-volume set of books, which includes a section about the Sacred Arrow at Noavose [1]

Today many Cheyenne people still go to fast at Noavose (Bear Butte) Pledges of fasting are made in times when loved ones are sick so that they will recover from their illnesses or other such reasons When family members are in the military, prayers are made there for their safe return home

Lately, Noavose has become endangered because of its potential for residential and commercial development and because of the proximity of the annual motorcycle rally in Sturgis, SD Northern Cheyenne and other tribes have come together to fight the development and the rally activities

DEER MEDICINE ROCKS

This site is located north of the Northern Cheyenne Reservation on private land It was where Hunkpapa Lakota Chief Sitting Bull went prior to the Battle of the Little Big Horn. He pledged his Sun Dance and vowed 100 pieces of his flesh offering to *Wakan Tanka* (the Lakota name of the creator). Sitting Bull's brother, Jumping Bull, cut 50 pieces of Sitting Bull's flesh from each of Sitting Bull's arms.

When Sitting Bull took his place in the Sun Dance lodge, blood ran down his arms and shoulders as he sat throughout the night. The next afternoon the crowd of people saw that Sitting Bull was weakening, and they laid him down on the ground.

The chief had a vision. Sitting Bull announced that he heard a voice saying, "I give you these because they have no ears." He looked up and saw soldiers and some Indians on horseback coming down like grasshoppers, with their heads down and their hats falling off. They were falling right into the camp. After that vision the Sun Dance came to an end, and the Hunkpapas moved toward the Little Big Horn. Thus the dream portended the results of the Cheyenne, Lakota, and Arapaho victory over George Armstrong Custer.[2]

In 1876, Lakota Chief Sitting Bull had a vision at Medicine Rocks. He looked up and saw soldiers and some Indians on horseback falling into the camp. (Photo by Heather Ryan)

LAKE DESMET

These accounts of Lake DeSmet are included here because they are rapidly being lost with the passage of time Only a few stories remain yet Lake DeSmet was once very central to the spiritual ceremonies of the Cheyenne people

The lake is located north of Buffalo, WY, a place where the Cheyenne would go for spiritual quests During one of these times Roman Nose, a famous Cheyenne warrior, fasted for four days and four nights with White Bull (or Ice as he was also known) White Bull served as Sitting Bull's medicine advisor According to a story that was relayed by one of the elders, Roman Nose was put out in the middle of the lake on a raft, and during the night the water creatures tried to get him

After some time it got very quiet, and he sensed something getting on his raft It was the weasel The weasel told him not to worry, he had chased those other creatures away who were trying to get him Weasel said he was the king of this lake and that he had come to instruct Roman Nose about some things before he went home

Weasel told Roman Nose to make a *parfleche* using the weasel's coat of fur The parfleche was to hold the weasel cap, some Arrows, and other medicine that the weasel taught Roman Nose Roman Nose, in his haste to join the battle, did not perform the necessary purification rites that would have restored the protective powers that had been granted him [3]

Roman Nose had been instructed by the weasel that the Arrows were to be used when an enemy was spotted These Arrows were to be thrown, and if they stuck in the ground, that meant they would defeat the enemy However, if the Arrows did not stick in the ground, the tribe was to move their camp The weasel cap was made for the chiefs to wear at their ceremonies The Arrows and weasel cap had powerful medicine and were kept in the parfleche

According to the elder relating this story, there is a photograph of Little Wolf wearing the weasel cap Prior to old man Wolf Road's death, he buried this parfleche somewhere in the hills south of Busby [4] White Bull made the buffalo-horned war bonnet that protected Roman Nose from enemy bullets That protective power was broken when a spoon made from the white man's metal touched the food Roman Nose was eating Shortly thereafter the Elk Society leader was shot down by Major George A Forsyth's men at Beecher's Island [5]

There is also a legend that some Cheyenne people went into the lake to escape the U S Cavalry This band of Cheyenne had camped near Lake DeSmet to replenish their supplies The men were hunting, and the women were drying meat and making moccasins and clothing before winter Soldiers had come upon them, and there was no place for the Cheyenne to escape since this area is in the open With no place to hide, they decided to go into the lake There were dogs that went into the lake with them Stories are told that sometimes a person can hear children playing on the water, dogs barking, or see people on the lake The Cheyenne honor these ancestors by taking prayer clothes and sending the cloth into the lake [6]

SACRED HAT

Esevone (the Sacred Buffalo Hat) is the great symbol and source of female renewing power Esevone's power renews the buffalo herds of the past, as well as the cattle herds of the present It was through the Buffalo Hat that the Sun Dance first came to the So'taahe people In the Sun Dance there is a Sacred Woman who offers her body as a renewal of the Cheyenne and their world Through the supernatural power of the Arrows and Buffalo Hat, the male and female relationships in Cheyenne life are blessed, ensuring continual strength, harmony, and new life for the people and their world [7]

SACRED ARROWS

The four sacred, black painted Arrows were given to Sweet Medicine at Bear Butte Cheyenne called the Arrows *Maahotse*, derived from the name of Ma'heo'o, the All Father These uniquely sacred objects share the supreme powers of the Creator himself, and they channel supernatural life into Cheyenne lives Maahotse continue to be the means by which the Cheyenne are united with the All Father After Morning Star's (Dull Knife's) village was destroyed by General McKenzie on November 1876, the Sacred Arrow Keeper, Black Hairy Dog bore the Arrows to safety in the south, and that is where they have remained The Sacred Arrows are the divinely-given symbol of male power, and no female dares to look at them [8]

1 Powell, P J (1969) *Sweet Medicine The continuing role of the Sacred Arrows the Sun Dance and the Sacred Buffalo Hat in Northern Cheyenne history* (Vol 1, p 19) Norman University of Oklahoma Press

2 Powell, P J , *Sweet Medicine*, p 111

3 Powell, P J , *Sweet Medicine*, p 95

4 Littlebear, R , (2005) DVD recording in Chief Dull Knife College library

5 Powell, P J , *Sweet Medicine*

6 E Whitedirt (personal communication, November 2007)

7 Powell, P J , *Sweet Medicine*

8 Powell P J , *Sweet Medicine*, p xxiii

Early Education on the
Northern Cheyenne Reservation

THOSE STEEPED IN European-based education often believe that people without formal schooling are uneducated. This is a misconception especially detrimental to American Indians. Before formal schooling was forced upon them, the Cheyenne and other tribes educated their children through a type of on-the-job training. Family members and elders were teachers of the Cheyenne children. The main instructors for children were aunts, uncles, and grandparents.

Children learned through observation in settings similar to today's "open classrooms," following the examples set by older tribal members. Education during the adolescent years became more intense and focused on preparing respected and productive adults, according to Henrietta Mann in her book on Cheyenne and Arapaho education. Subject areas such as language, ceremonies, tribal government, customs, gender roles, traditions, morals, botany, biology, astronomy, geography, child rearing, hunting, weaponry, food preservation, nutrition, agriculture, bead work, tanning hides, sewing, healing/medicine, making clothing, keeping a lodge, and religion were taught by extended family and tribal members.

Traditional oral storytelling was performed by certain respected elders. Stories were divided up into narratives about the creation, prophets, tribal history, mysteries, heroes, and war stories. The Cheyenne curriculum was culturally applicable and promoted life-long learning and survival.[1]

With the onset of the reservation period, educational practices underwent a drastic change as the following accounts detail.

FORT MARION PRISON, FLORIDA

In 1875, Lt. Richard Henry Pratt escorted 72 Indian warriors suspected of murdering white settlers to Fort Marion Prison in St. Augustine, FL. The warriors consisted primarily of Kiowas, Cheyennes, and Arapahos The captives included one woman, a Cheyenne by the name of Buffalo Calf (*No-chi*) They were held captive in an attempt to keep their tribes peaceful [2] Pratt later became one of the most aggressive crusaders for assimilation education, founding the Carlisle Indian School in Pennsylvania and adopting the motto, "kill the Indian to save the man " Through education and humane treatment, Pratt believed that even the most "savage" of Indians might become educated and law abiding citizens

He viewed the imprisonment of the warriors at Fort Marion as an opportunity to begin his experiment He put the men in uniform and had them perform military drills The prisoners learned to read and write lessons in English Christian religious instruction was also part of the rigorous routine Pratt called the warriors the "Florida Boys " They referred to Pratt as "Captain" even though his rank was lieutenant Out of the 72 prisoners, there were 33 Cheyennes The Cheyenne prisoners held at Fort Marion were

Heap of Birds *Ve'keseoxhaestoxese*
Bear Shield *Nahkoheose*
Eagle's Head *Netseheme'ko*
Medicine Water *Ma'heonemahpe*
Long Back *Tsehe'ese'pa'o*
Hail Stone *Ao'eseto*
Rising Bull *Hotoa'asetoesestse*
Limpy *Nohne'kaheso*
Bear's Heart *Nahkohehesta*
Star *Hotohke*
Howling Wolf *Ho'nehenestoohe*
Making Medicine *Hoxehetane*
Antelope *Vo'aa'e*
Wolf's Marrow *O'kohomehevene*
Little Medicine *Ma'heo'oxhaahketa*
Shave Head *Oo'kestseahe*
Roman Nose *Vohko'xenehe*
Big Nose *Tahpe'ee'ese*
Squint Eye *Tšeške'ehaenehe*
Little Chief *Veho Oxhaahketahtse*
Match *Tšehešehaseo'o*
Buffalo Meat *Ho'evoo'otse*
Buzzard *Oo'hehe*
Soaring Eagle *Netseóhnema'e'áhtse*
Bear Killer *Nahkohkena'hane*
Left Hand *Namosestse*
Chief Killer *Na'haneveho*
Buffalo Calf *Voestae'keso*
Gray Beard *Vohpeme'hahtse*

90

Big Moccasin: *Ma'xeheseeo'otse*
Lean Bear: *Nahko Oxhaahketáhtse*
Standing Wolf: *Ho'nehe Onee'estse*
Spotted Elk: *Mo'cohvovo'haestse*

While in captivity the men were encouraged by Lt. Pratt to make souvenirs to sell to the tourists who wintered in Florida. The prisoners also painted and made drawings of their experiences at Fort Marion. The drawings and souvenirs were sold in the region, and the prisoners were allowed to keep the money from the sales. Many sent money home to help their families financially. The men also performed dances and skits for the tourists. These performances were said to be real crowd pleasers with locals and tourists. The group of prisoners became quite famous and earned a reputation as a popular tourist attraction.

By the end of 1883, Fort Marion discharged all of the prisoners in Florida for lack of funding. The men felt betrayed and deceived by the government, but some of them later achieved success and led productive lives. Most returned to Indian Territory (Oklahoma), but several went to Hampton Institute in Virginia. Those

By late 1878 Pratt was told he could continue the education of the prisoners being released from Fort Marion. He took these prisoners to Hampton Normal and Industrial Institute in Virginia, a school for freed slaves. These men were accustomed to the restrictive style of clothing, spoke English, and had converted to Christianity. After years of working among whites, they had fewer problems adapting to change and separation from families than students who came later. Pratt was famous for his "before and after" photographs. Many "after" photographs resembled this picture of posed students with props of books and tools. Pictured are 12 of the "Florida Boys" with the tools of civilization. (Courtesy of Hampton University Archives)

who returned to Indian Territory overcame many obstacles Often the men were met with distrust by tribal members People criticized their appearance and new ways Buffalo Meat eventually became a deacon of a Baptist church and served as head chief of the Southern Cheyenne Before landing the deacon position he wrote a letter to Pratt saying he longed for the Florida days when he was never hungry or poor, and the white people were his friends He said his clothes were badly worn, and he would not receive new clothing for a long time [5] In Oklahoma, Buffalo Meat, Bear Killer, Chief Killer, Hail Stone, and Star are known to have worked at various jobs, wherever they could find employment The men farmed, raised cattle, cut wood, dug wells, made bricks, and became leaders in their communities

Upon his release from Fort Marion, the Cheyenne named John Tichkematse (Squint Eyes) went on to study at Hampton Institute Later he became an employee of the Smithsonian Institution, working in various departments There he was trained in taxidermy and learned to display birds and mammals He collected bird specimens for the museum He traveled with anthropologist Frank Cushing to study the Native people of New Mexico, Florida, and Arizona He later served in the cavalry and police forces before settling in Lame Deer, MT While in Montana he took up ranching and became an active member of the Mennonite church

Several of the men went on to further their education after their release Roman Nose helped to organize the Roman Nose Gypsum Company in 1903 Others hired out as scouts Many returned home where they joined police forces, organized ceremonial dances, founded Christian missions, created local businesses, taught at agency schools, farmed, ranched, headed tribal councils, and preserved traditional societies However, the whereabouts of many warriors could not be traced, according to Lookingbill A strong bond was created amongst the men during their banishment These men gathered courage through their exile and were the trail blazers to a new and foreign movement They met many challenges and—most importantly—refused to become culturally extinct

BOARDING SCHOOLS

One of the most damaging and catastrophic federal Indian policies was the enforcement of boarding school education for Native Americans, and the impacts are still being felt today Beginning in 1884, Cheyenne children at a very young age were forcibly taken from their families and taken to the Catholic boarding school, St Labre Indian School, at Ashland, MT, just off the reservation This was the year that the Northern Cheyenne Reservation was formed, and the people were forced to live a sedentary, non-warlike lifestyle This was a complete change

PLATE TWELVE: WAR DANCE AT FORT MARION

The performances pictured by Cohoe were so popular that people started lining up at 7 p.m. to rush to the fort. Over 2,000 spectators at one time reportedly watched the performances. The dancers performed the War Dance of the Plains Indians, a striking contrast with the Victorian ladies and gentlemen with their bustles, fans, suits, and top hats. (Reprinted with permission of University of Oklahoma Press)

from their former culture. An Indian Bureau school opened at Busby on the reservation in 1904, the Tongue River Boarding School.

St. Labre Indian School began with a humanitarian purpose. It was opened by Bishop John Brondel, the Vicar Apostolic of Helena, MT. A soldier stationed at Fort Keogh in Miles City had contacted the bishop because he was concerned about the poor living conditions of the Northern Cheyenne Indians. On April 3, 1884, the first mass was held at St. Labre Mission, which was named after St. Benedict Joseph Labre. [6] The mission provided two meals a day, and after an early supper the children were dismissed.[7] Some of the parents accompanied their children to school and stayed all day until school was let out.[8] Some of the parents refused to send their children to St Labre because "there is too much praying and talking of Christ," according to Indian Bureau Agent J. Tully. Tully told his supervisors in Washington, DC, however, that he knew how to enforce school attendance: "first by persuasion and then by withholding harness and other goods sent here for issue to them."[9]

The goals for teachers at both schools included religious conversion as well as education. In a letter written in 1940 by Principal Jerry N. Thompson of the Tongue River Boarding School at Busby to the superintendent of the Tongue River Agency, he said, "All boarding pupils were lined up on the porches of the dormitory on Sunday morning and from there marched under the direction of a teacher to the church of their choice for Sunday school from 10:00 a.m. to 11:00 a.m. Then they marched back to the dormitory after services ended."[10]

The school standards usually included getting Natives to dress, speak, and look like white people. Their hair was cut; their diet changed; and their language, religion, and culture were suppressed. The boarding school program was designed to remove traditional culture, family patterns, and communal behaviors.[11] The children were immediately confronted with a language barrier and were removed from their families and all that was familiar. Unaccustomed to separations from family and home, they became quite homesick and often became physically ill. The children could not acclimatize to the regimentation and were often overcome with depression. School attendance was a problem throughout the years. Parental resistance to the acculturation took on different forms, such as refusing to send

The girls from the Tongue River Boarding school in Busby are standing in front of the Mennonite church. The students were required to go to church. (Photo from the Mennonite Collection)

children to school, sending orphaned or less desirable children, complaining to agents, and reinforcing tribal customs during home visits [12]

An Indian Compulsory Attendance Law was passed by Congress in 1891 Indian Bureau agents were responsible for school attendance and keeping schools filled The Secretary of Interior was empowered to withhold rations and annuities if children did not attend school One of the most harmful ideas for solving the attendance problem was separating children and their families for longer periods of time Advocates of boarding schools argued that educational training, in combination with several years of separation from family would diminish tribal customs and take care of school absenteeism The separation from family was the foundation of Lt Pratt's educational philosophies

As a result, it became the policy of boarding schools to limit home visits Children were allowed to go home for only one weekend a month at the Tongue River Boarding School and St Labre Boarding School Some students and families remember the school as being their only source of food and shelter Nevertheless, they were devastated by long-term effects of the students' separation from family and community Home visits were regulated by school officials, and if the school considered a child's home unsuitable for any reason, parents were denied permission to have their children visit Loss of family contact during childhood created a hardship on children and families Some parents voluntarily placed their children in school, whereas others evaded or opposed the mandatory enrollment

In some situations parents went to great lengths to hide children and make false claims of sickness to protect and keep their children home

> James Deafy has two children enrolled in the Busby School According to custom they are allowed to go home over week ends once each month They were given this privilege at their regular time, but a week later their mother came for them to go home again The principal told her that they had been home the week before The mother contended that it was their time now, and after considerable argument, she took the children against the principal's protest
>
> The principal did not feel justified in using physical means to prevent her, and she took the children against his protest He phoned the superintendent who advised him to have the police go that evening and tell Mrs Deafy that she would have to appear before Indian court at Lame Deer the next day She should be ready when police called in the morning
>
> She told the policeman positively that she would not go to Lame Deer During the night the husband missed her from the house and went in search of her He found her in a small outbuilding hanging from the rafter with a rope around her neck The husband hastily cut the rope but it was sometime before they were sure she would live This incident indicates to what extremes some of the parents will go to have their way about the children attending school [13]

Parents were, also aware of the health risks of enrolling their children in boarding schools where they could be exposed to serious contagious diseases Communicable diseases thrived in overcrowded and communal environments of reservation boarding schools In 1930 the Tongue River Boarding School located at Busby suffered from crowded conditions in the dormitories Tongue River Agency Superintendent C B Lohmiller wrote a letter April 29, 1930, to the Commissioner of Indian Affairs describing the deplorable living arrangements He said, "The small dormitory for boys measured 28 5 by 16 5 feet, and 19 boys sleep in 10 beds The beds are single size, and two boys sleep in each bed The larger dormitory for boys measures 39 5 by 32 5 feet and has 12 single-size beds and sleeps 21 boys. In the dormitory for small girls, 24 girls sleep in 12 single size beds The total dormitory should house 68 students, but 83 students sleep in the dormitories "[14]

Tongue River Agency Supervisor George Miller wrote a report on Education on the Tongue River Reservation Nov 30, 1928, describing the health crisis where 44% of the children at the Tongue River Boarding School had trachoma and 52% of the pupils at the Birney Day School had it (Trachoma is a chronic contagious bacterial condition that can result in blindness if untreated) He described horrific conditions at the boarding school

> The laundress and the poorly equipped laundry the past few months probably help to account for the soiled condition of the children's clothing The lack of a supply of both hot and cold water was mentioned in section one of this report Boys washing in a dark room, without warm water, can't be expected to get very clean No individual combs were used by either boys or girls On the boys' side of the building no toothbrushes were to be found Ventilation of the dormitories and classrooms was fairly good but the whole building has an unsanitary odor This is due to lack of careful cleaning, especially in corners, and to unsanitary plumbing—clogged toilets and drain pipes [15]

Tuberculosis was also a huge problem Pupils with contagious diseases were theoretically excluded from attending school, but tuberculosis, trachoma, and other diseases thrived in classrooms and overcrowded dormitories The diseases became a threat to not only boarding school students but also to the reservation population Students returning home often spread the sicknesses to family members According to statistics taken in 1911 by the Commissioner of Indian Affairs, 31% of the population on the Tongue River Reservation had tuberculosis and nearly 17% had trachoma [16]

Correspondence between Superintendent Boggess and the Commissioner of Indian Affairs in Washington, DC, dated 1923 states "I feel that our physician is giving more careful attention to the children excused from school than any other physician we have had here I keep a record of the excused children and from time to time, we discuss the cases So many of these are tubercular that there is no hope of returning a large percentage of them to the class room."[17] Tuberculosis remained the greatest health problem on the reservation as late as 1947 In a report prepared by Dr H W Kassel and Field Nurse Miss Francis Cleave they said statistics indicated that 800 deaths per 100,000 population were due to tuberculosis Venereal disease and trachoma were still prevalent and special care and precautions were being taken to prevent an increase.[18]

"Vocational" Training at the Boarding Schools

Congress never appropriated enough money to fully support the reservation schools The lack of funding resulted in the overcrowding and contributed to the spread of disease It also meant that the schools utilized student labor to subsidize the daily operations Pupils assisted with building repairs, washed and ironed laundry, fixed uniforms, milked cows grew and harvested crops, cleaned, hauled water and coal, and participated in kitchen duties

At the time, the administrators believed they were providing the children with skills that would help them be productive members of mainstream society

> So far as developing the boys into farmers, one of the most gratifying endeavors of the Busby School is that 10 Indian boys were given 5 heifers, and they stayed at the school all summer and looked after those heifers, raised feed for them, and otherwise took care of them This is the first time that has happened in this school They were also given a sow each, and the results have been an average of 8 pigs to the sow Now if that isn't getting the lads started in the right direction, I do not know what a right start would be In general the school has produced its own potatoes, beef, pork, and milk, and in addition 1,000 bushels of grains such as wheat, rye, barley, and oats and much alfalfa [19]

At the Tongue River Boarding School, the supervisor of home economics, Carrie A Lyford, described her program with much enthusiasm in a letter dated March 11, 1936

> The children are learning good habits of work through the limited amount of detail work carried on The girls mend, iron, cook, and clean The boys clean, milk, carry wood, and do other errands All the older boarding school girls report to the sewing room in small groups for 10 week periods They hem towels, sheets, and pillow cases and make holders, bloomers, night gowns, aprons, and school dresses
>
> All the girls, both day and boarding pupils, join the 4-H Club after they are ten years old Each of these girls sews one-half day each week on carefully graded problems, following the Montana 4-H Club program Each girl has a box in which she keeps her work carefully, and she takes it to her home or room to do homework The girls are taken to Billings to select their patterns

and materials Their shopping trip marks an eventful day for them When they go to Billings, they are taken to various places of interest as well as to the dry goods stores

They are also taken once a year to the reservation Achievement Day a few go to the county Achievement Day Once a year they entertain the Boy Scouts at a party which they plan In the late spring those who have completed their work creditably are taken on a camping expedition The girls are learning poise and confidence and are having very happy times [20]

Looking back at the boarding schools, Indian educators today point out that much of the trades training for boys and domestic training for girls was not really "vocational" training It did not provide the job skills necessary for employment Students learned skills that were useful, but much of the labor was tedious and dull A small percentage of the students actually made a living at the trade they learned in school [21]

1 Mann H (1997) *Cheyenne Arapaho education 1871-1982* Niwot University Press of Colorado

2 Lookingbill B (2006) *War dance at Fort Marion Plains Indian war prisoners* Norman, OK University of Oklahoma Press

3 Lookingbill, *War dance at Fort Marion*

4 Lookingbill, *War dance at Fort Marion*

5 Lookingbill, *War dance at Fort Marion*

6 Little Bear, R E (1983) *History of Northern Cheyenne education* p 6 Available at Chief Dull Knife College Library at Lame Deer, MT

7 Schonenbach, M A (n d) *History of St Labre Mission* pp 1-2 Available at Chief Dull Knife College Library at Lame Deer, MT

8 Roth, M J (1966) *Education contributions of St Labres Mission to the Cheyenne Indians* p 2 Available at Chief Dull Knife College Library at Lame Deer MT

9 Tully, I (1884, June 30) Monthly Report on the Tongue River Agency McCracken Library, Buffalo Bill Historical Museum p 4

10 Thompson, J (1940, Feb 13) Letter on religious instruction at the Tongue River Boarding School Letter received by Office of Indian Affairs, Record Group 4, Proselytizing Files 8NS07597013 National Archives and Records Administration, Denver, CO

11 Davis, J (2001) American Indian boarding school experiences Recent studies from Native perspectives *Magazine of History*, 15(2), 20-22

12 Davis, American Indian boarding school experiences

13 Stevens, C, supervisor of schools Monthly Report, April 15 to May 1, 1923 Report received by Office of Indian Affairs Record Group 3, Classified Files, 8NS07597010 National Archives and Records Administration Denver CO

14 Lohmiller, C B, Superintendent of Tongue River Agency (1930, April 29) Inspection Report received by Commissioner of Indian Affairs, Washington, DC, Record Group 75, Records of the Bureau of Indian Affairs 1926-1952, 10NS-075-97-013 National Archives and Records Administration, Denver, CO

15 Miller G I Supervisor of Indian Schools (1928, Nov 30) Report on Education received by Commissioner of Indian Affairs Washington DC, Record Group 75, Records of the Bureau of Indian Affairs, 1926-1952, 10NS-075-97-013 National Archives and Records Administration, Denver, CO

16 United States Department of the Interior June 30, 1911 Annual Report of the Commissioner of Indian Affairs, p 152

17 Letter on education/health matters at the Tongue River Boarding School, April 11, 1923 Letter received by Commissioner of Indian Affairs, Washington DC Record Group 9, General Correspondence Files, 0NS-075-97-010 National Archives and Records Administration, Denver, CO

18 Kassel H W & Cleave, K I (1947, July 29) Report on health issues on the Tongue River Agency received by Commissioner of Indian Affairs, Washington, D C, McCracken Research Library Buffalo Bill Research Museum Cody, WY

19 Letter on education/health matters at the Tongue River Boarding School, September 10 1940 Letter received by Commissioner Indian Affairs, Washington DC, McCracken Research Library, Buffalo Bill Research Museum, Cody, WY

20 Inlord, C A (1936, March 16) Report on education at the Tongue River Boarding School received by Commissioner of Indian Affairs, Washington, DC, Record Group 75 Bureau of Indian Affairs Files, 1926-1956, 10NS-075-97-013, National Archives and Records Administration, Denver CO

21 Archuleta M L, Child B J & Lomawaima K I (2000) *Away from home American Indian boarding school experiences* Phoenix, AZ Heard Museum

THE NORTHERN CHEYENNE leaders Chief Dull Knife and Dr John Woodenlegs were important advocates for education for the Northern Cheyenne, and both helped to encourage schooling on the reservation Chief Dull Knife emphasized the importance of schools in 1878 even before the Northern Cheyenne had their own reservation [1] A century later, Woodenlegs said, "The time is past when we have to keep living in some old, broken down way Education is the key to our future "[2]

Their efforts to help the Cheyenne learn a new way of life were not intended to support assimilation or replace the students' Cheyenne culture Instead, they wanted to obtain the resources needed for the Cheyenne to survive in a society dominated by the non-Indian, American culture Among the many issues to which Northern Cheyenne leaders have devoted their energy, education has been the toughest in which to achieve success Yet the Northern Cheyennes now are beginning to see the benefits of schooling that Chief Dull Knife and John Woodenlegs envisioned

Attitudes toward education today continue to be shaped by the history of education on the Northern Cheyenne Reservation Among the most important factors affecting schooling today are the legacy of the early boarding schools, which eventually led Cheyenne leaders to pursue greater influence and control over local schooling and to minimize the effects of racism on students and parents Another important factor is the persistent poverty on the reservation One might well say that Custer did less violence to the Cheyenne people than a hundred years of poverty Nearly 40% of Northern Cheyenne families live under the poverty level, which was exacerbated in 2007 by $3-per-gallon gasoline and the remoteness of the Northern Cheyenne homeland (about a hundred miles from an urban center) According to the 2000 census, unemployment fluctuated from 60-85%, for jobs are scarce and often seasonal on the Northern Cheyenne Reservation Almost

42% of the reservation's people were under the age of 18, and another 50% were between the ages of 18 and 64 [5]

Like students in other reservation communities where job opportunities are scarce, many Cheyenne high school students need help to deal with peer pressure regarding substance abuse, overcome poor preparation for the demands of high school, access the academic resources needed to succeed, take care of family and financial needs, and see the relevance of high school graduation to their future opportunities These are the daunting conditions that Cheyenne educators must address

The 1960s and the 1970s were a critical time in the history of Indian education and the Northern Cheyennes had an important role During this time, a national movement for greater tribal control of schooling was supported by legislation in 1965 (Title I of the Elementary and Secondary Education Act) and 1972 (the Indian Education Act) The Northern Cheyenne Tribe assumed control of the governance and the facilities of the Bureau of Indian Affairs (BIA) school in Busby in 1972, making it one of the first in the nation to provide its children schooling through a contract between the BIA and the tribal council

In the same year, the tribe established a vocational education program, which three years later was chartered as one of the nation's first tribal colleges Chief Dull Knife College was granted full accreditation by the Northwest Commission on Colleges and Universities in 1995 Then the community initiated another first—a public high school in Lame Deer These successes demonstrate that when the Northern Cheyenne decide to tackle an issue about which they are deeply concerned, they do it in a big way And they usually succeed

Overview

Over the last several decades, Northern Cheyenne educational achievement has increased dramatically among adults By 1980, the majority of Northern Cheyenne adults (55%) had completed high school At this time, Northern Cheyenne high school education was keeping pace with schooling among American Indians across the country even though it was still lower than for residents of Montana generally (74%) In 1980 only a small percentage (3%) of the Northern Cheyenne had completed a college degree, compared to 18% of all Montanans

Similar to national patterns, education has generally increased with each new generation of Northern Cheyenne For example, the 1989 Northern Cheyenne Educational Census [4] showed that just 20% of Cheyennes 65 years or older and half of adults ages 45-64 had completed 12 years of schooling at that time Importantly, among the next younger group of adults (ages 25-44), 80% had achieved 12 years of schooling

However, unlike the majority of Americans, the Northern Cheyenne have recently seen increasing dropout rates among their youth and young adults. Only two thirds (66%) of young adult Northern Cheyennes (ages 19-24) had completed 12 years of school by 1989, and less than 60% of high school seniors were graduating.[5] Unfortunately, the dropout rate has remained high since the early 1990s. Other American Indians across the nation also have experienced this decline in the levels of schooling among young adults.[6] The implications of high dropout rates are serious for reservation schools, which now must find new ways to help students finish high school and become eligible for college and other post-secondary education.

Such changes are related to the different opportunities and conditions of schooling that each generation has faced. Earlier generations sometimes lacked schools to attend. When the Northern Cheyenne Educational Census was conducted in 1989, some older Cheyennes reported that they only received a third grade education because there were no higher grades to attend. Several of these people even went to the third grade several times because they wanted to continue to go to school.

In the past, Northern Cheyenne leaders fought to increase schooling opportunities at every level. The Northern Cheyenne are now served by several types of schools—private, tribal, and public—that provide a range of pre-kindergarten to 12 schooling opportunities. With the accreditation of Chief Dull Knife College, the educational circle was completed for providing education opportunities from preschool to at least two years of higher education. These schools now are trying to increase resources to help Northern Cheyenne students stay in school until they graduate and continue to college.

Each of the four school districts serving the reservation is described in the following sections: St. Labre Catholic Mission School, Northern Cheyenne Tribal School (formerly known as Busby Tribal School), Colstrip Public School, and Lame Deer High School.

ST. LABRE CATHOLIC MISSION SCHOOL

Both Catholic and Mennonite missions were established initially to educate and "assimilate" the Northern Cheyenne. However, only the St. Labre Catholic Mission in Ashland, MT, (just east of the reservation) has offered both day school and boarding facilities. It serves both Northern Cheyenne and Crow Indian students. St. Labre Catholic School is still part of the St. Labre Mission founded a century ago. It is a privately administered Roman Catholic school, which serves an almost exclusively Indian population. The Northern Cheyenne students are primarily from Ashland and Lame Deer communities. St. Labre is probably the best known of the schools serving the reservation because of its successful national direct-mail, fund-raising activities Once an impoverished mission, over the last several decades it has built a large and relatively stable endowment from private donations

As a Catholic school, St Labre emphasizes spiritual as well as academic development The history of St Labre closely parallels national priorities in Indian policy In the earlier years of its history, missionaries at St Labre favored assimilation Older Cheyennes relate how some tribal members, inspired by the sermons of St Labre missionaries, roamed the reservation on horseback, roping and pulling down sweat lodges While some recall harsh or negative experiences in this boarding school, others express gratitude for the care they received during difficult times on the reservation [8]

Today, St Labre staff integrates Roman Catholic values with respect for the traditions of the community Now some St Labre clergy participate in sweat lodge activities with members of their parish Due to its commitment to provide educational programs with private funding, St Labre does not allowed federally funded special education programs to be offered However, it does provide some remedial instruction with the intent to mainstream students as quickly as possible

An important part of St Labre school's history is the changes in governance in 1978 From 1978 through 1984 St Labre School operated under a contract with the Bureau of Indian Affairs During that time, the school was governed by a community-elected school board, and the facilities were leased from the St Labre Mission In 1985, however, the governance was again assumed by the Catholic diocese of Great Falls MT A community advisory board, elected mostly from the Northern Cheyenne Reservation area but including one member from the Crow Tribe, provided input to the school management [9]

Funding for the school improved radically when it became a private Catholic school again As a contract school, it received federal monies of about $400,000 per year, but with the change to private status, its budget increased to $1 7 million At that time, St Labre charged a minimal tuition but had a scholarship program for students in need In 1985 the composition of the faculty and staff was primarily non-Indian,[10] there was one Cheyenne and one Sioux teacher, one Cheyenne counselor and 15 Cheyenne paraprofessionals In 2007 the enrollment at St Labre was about 500 students, with about 210 elementary students, 120 middle school students, and 150 high school students

In the 1980s and early 1990s, between a third and a half of the students attending St Labre Catholic Mission School were from the Crow reservation, located just west of the Northern Cheyenne Reservation Today over 90% of the students at St Labre are Native American, and of those 62% are Northern Cheyenne [11] The high school continues to be accredited by the Northwest Association of Schools and Colleges Some of the classes offered at St Labre are home economics, business, music, art, Native American literature, history and tribal governments, Native language, and culture [12]

In recent years, some members of Northern Cheyenne Tribe have felt that St Labre Mission should share the money they have made off of the "plight and poverty" of the people [13] In 2004, St Labre brought in $27 million in contributions through donations, and its assets from investments, buildings, and land amounted to $89 4 million [14]

Dr Jeffrey Sanders a professor at Montana State University-Billings, said, " There is often friction on reservations between mission and boarding schools and some tribal members Although some mission schools are remembered for positive contributions, many tribal members have been left with bad feelings over abuse, the dismissal of Native cultures, or other problems For many Indians, mission schools or boarding schools represent the symbol of majority culture trying to forcefully assimilate a Native people "[15] Controversy over the mission resources has continued in recent years

BUSBY TRIBAL SCHOOL

As tribes won the right to provide educational services to their members in 1972 under the Indian Education Act, the Northern Cheyenne Tribe contracted with the BIA to administer the school at Busby Its governance became the responsibility of an interim all Cheyenne school board, according to Dr Richard Little Bear, who was elected to the first school board [16] It was one of the first BIA schools in the country to be converted to an Indian-controlled school Tribal members had been upset about conditions in the school In its early years as a boarding school administered by the BIA, strict and sometimes abusive policies were directed at the students [17] The unhealthy conditions of the 1920s and 1930s were described in the previous chapter In 1969, the conditions were still very bad

Daniel M Rosenfelt[18] summarized the conditions at the BIA boarding and day school, which served 98 boarders and 223 elementary and secondary day students [19] Consultants to the Senate Subcommittee reported to U S Sen Edward M Kennedy that "the Busby School, both day and boarding students, seems to be operating as a custodial institution " Further, the school was reputed to have an unusually high suicide attempt rate [20]

Rosenfelt described the process of developing the tribally controlled school First they had to bridge the barriers between the community and the school This effort was aided by the parent participation requirements of Title I, and a "Parental Involvement Program in Education" project funded by the Donner Foundation of New York Gradually, he said, a consensus formed among the community that it, rather than the BIA, should operate the Busby School The BIA, in turn, seemed eager to relinquish control of the school In July 1972 an elected Busby School Board assumed control of the school under a $795,000 contract [21] Thus, the tribe changed the BIA's Tongue River Reservation Boarding School to Busby Tribal School

The first chairman of the Indian-controlled school board was Ted Risingsun He was eager to transform the school from the assimilationist school that he remembered from his youth during the 1930s

> Everything was like in the military I was a little boy, and with the other little boys, we would get up when the whistle blew, dress when the whistle blew, go out and "police" the grounds picking up little pieces of paper and things so we would learn to be "responsible" We were punished if we spoke to each other in Cheyenne, and we were made to feel ashamed that we were Indians and ashamed of our families When I got a chance to go home, I cried that I did not want to come back [to school] But my family said that I must go back So I became deaf I have been told that it was not a physical problem, but hysterical deafness But I could not hear, and my family could not send me back to the school I still, today, have trouble with my hearing sometimes I think it goes back to what happened to me as a child The Indian schools have done terrible things to Indian children [22]

Risingsun described being forbidden to speak his Native language "I'd never spoken English, but at school I was expected to use it I didn't even know that my name [in English] was Ted Risingsun I hung my head If there had been a bilingual [or multi-cultural] teacher there, things would have been different "[23]

Busby School has changed a great deal With more control by the tribe, it has become more responsive to community concerns and teaches Cheyenne students more about their history, culture, and language However, it has continued to face problems in providing the kinds of schooling Cheyenne students need Busby Tribal School's unique mandate to provide schooling to any Cheyenne student who wants to attend has resulted in a large number of students from other communities on the reservation choosing to go there, overtaxing the school

Among the three schools serving the reservation in the 1980s, Busby Tribal School had the smallest resource base with which to provide comprehensive services for grades K through 12 [24] For example, in the 1985-86 school year, Busby Tribal School received only about $650,000 from the BIA for administration of the school and about $332,000 in federal grants for special programs such as bilingual education, special education, and Title IV Indian education

Busby Tribal School's enrollment declined dramatically from 207 in 1972 to 80 students in 1985 Declines in the early 1980s were related to the school being closed because the building was assessed as hazardous, there was not enough funding for adequate maintenance [25] During this time, Busby Tribal School was governed by a five-person board elected within the portion of the reservation located in Big Horn County, the westernmost part of the reservation. Students attending Busby Tribal School were primarily from Busby, but a substantial proportion was bussed from Lame Deer. Dropout rates estimated in the late 1980s was 54%.[26] In recent years, the school changed its name to Northern Cheyenne Tribal School to more accurately reflect its mission to serve the entire reservation. In 2007, enrollment had climbed again to about 175 students. Both Northern Cheyenne and Crow students attend the school.

Colstrip Public School

Colstrip grew from a small settlement to a boom town during the energy boom of the early 1970s, as discussed in the energy chapter. Twenty-two miles north of the reservation, Colstrip is in one of the state's wealthiest school districts. It prides itself on an abundance of academic and athletic facilities and a wide variety of learning opportunities for its students. Colstrip schools are governed by a six-member school board elected district-wide, with one board member elected from the Northern Cheyenne Reservation. Faculty and staff composition in the 1980s included 51 teachers and staff in the high school. Only three American Indians worked for the school district, one as a counselor, one as the home school coordinator, and one as an elementary teacher.[27]

The budget for Colstrip High School increased from a little under a million dollars in 1980 to over $2.8 million in 1985 as a result of Public Law 874 (which authorized funding for reservation students in lieu of taxes from residents) and from the Johnson-O'Malley program (which provided special funding to school districts with Indian student enrollments).[28] When this law went into effect, the public school district in Colstrip admitted increasing numbers of Northern Cheyenne students. Colstrip's student body reflects the population of the town and surrounding area, which is primarily white, middle- and working-class. Livelihoods of these families include primarily mining-related work, service jobs, and ranching.

In the late 1980s about a third of the students were from the Northern Cheyenne Reservation, primarily from Lame Deer, although there were students from Busby as well. Some students lived as far as 75 miles from the school. Although the Indian students comprised a minority of the student body, the Indian students at Colstrip represented the single largest concentration of Indian students in the three schools serving most reservation residents at that time.

Enrollment of Indian students in the high school has typically ranged from 28% to 38% of the total high school enrollment. Total enrollment in Colstrip High School declined sharply between 1982 and 1989, primarily because of the end of construction on local power plants. High school enrollment was as high as 452 in 1985, but it decreased by more than half by 1987. Enrollment in Colstrip High School also was affected by the establishment of Lame Deer High School in the 1990s, which drew away some Northern Cheyenne students. Enrollment increased again in later years. In fall 2006 enrollment in Colstrip High School was 231, and 422 students were enrolled in the elementary schools.

LAME DEER PUBLIC SCHOOLS

Since 1909 the town of Lame Deer has had a public school district that served elementary and junior high students. In the 1940s, two buildings housed the kindergarten through 8th grades in Lame Deer.[29] While the early schooling provided by the Lame Deer School District was primarily intended to assimilate students, Lame Deer Schools subsequently increased the focus on Northern Cheyenne history and culture in the curriculum and hired Northern Cheyenne teachers and teacher aides. Northern Cheyenne members of the school board represent community needs and interests for the benefit of students.

Starting in the 1960s, the Northern Cheyenne initiated efforts to add a high school to the Lame Deer Public School District, pointing out the excessive bussing and the high drop out rates (42-54%) for its students who traveled to other high schools.[30] Lame Deer was the only area of its size in the entire state without a public high school; each of the other six reservations in the state had one. Some rural students were bussed as far as 150 miles daily to attend classes in Colstrip, Hardin, Busby, or Ashland. Some students did not want to attend St. Labre Catholic School in Ashland, 23 miles from Lame Deer, Busby Tribal School, located 16 miles from Lame Deer, or Colstrip public schools, 22 miles from Lame Deer.

During most recent decades, the largest concentration of Northern Cheyenne students has attended Colstrip schools. Typically up to 30% of students enrolled in the Colstrip public schools have been Cheyenne. Nevertheless, the Northern Cheyenne dropout study report[31] showed that about 42% of Cheyenne students dropped out of Colstrip High School compared to only 8% of white students. Although students attending Colstrip High School typically had more courses to choose from and some services for American Indian students, they also reportedly experienced more prejudice and discrimination than at other local schools. Native Studies were not offered at Colstrip until recently.[32]

Gail Small, then a teenager, remembered what it was like to attend the high school in Colstrip during the boom years. "We were really treated badly as Indian students," she said. "They called us 'prairie niggers,' everything you can imagine. We had to really fight just to hold our ground."[33] While Small went on to graduate from the University of Montana and to get a law degree from the University of

Oregon, the high school experience never left her memory. She founded Native Action in Lame Deer in 1984, and the organization later fought for the local high school.

Native Action became involved after its youth organizer, Jay Wolf Black, surveyed young people and discovered that a high school was their number one priority. Native Action presented petitions signed by high school parents to the two county school superintendents. One of the Native Action's donors, Archie Alexander, a retired administrative lawyer, volunteered to be the lead attorney. Indian school superintendents from around the country donated their time as expert witnesses. The local school board, the tribal government, and the school superintendent worked together for the new high school, but they were opposed by all the neighboring school districts. Every Indian child was worth $10,000 in federal impact aid; the new high school threatened to take millions from the other schools, according to Small. After the new district was created, Congress allocated $7.3 million to build a permanent facility.[34]

After a lengthy effort, the Montana Office of Public Instruction approved the establishment of a public high school district in Lame Deer in 1994. This decision required Congressional approval for the federal funds to build the school. When the high school was built, students who had previously quit school re-enrolled to complete their education.[35] Having a public high school in Lame Deer now means that Cheyenne students no longer have to leave their community or reservation to receive a public education.

Despite its successful beginning, Lame Deer High School has faced many of the same challenges faced by the other high schools in ensuring that students stay in school and graduate. Students' skepticism about schooling can be traced to the negative school experiences of family and community members in the boarding school era as well as contemporary prejudice. Students in all the schools also suffer from poor preparation in early years, leading to frustration and failure in high school, distraction from schooling related to substance abuse and peer groups, and perceptions of the irrelevance of school credentials to getting good-paying jobs in the local economy.[36] Additionally, students are negatively affected by the high turnover levels of staff and teachers that are characteristic of schools on the reservation.[37] Such changes contribute to a lack of continuity in instruction in core subjects such as math and science that are critical for school success and college preparation. Parents continue to worry about the lack of student motivation, poor school performance, and drug and alcohol use.[38]

In fact, dropout rates at Lame Deer High School have been as high as at the other local high schools. Lame Deer High School's dropout rate is suggested by the high school completion rates reported by the Montana Office of Public Instruction. The completion rate at Lame Deer High School was 48% in 2003, 45%

in 2004, and 56% in 2005 According to these figures, about the same number of Northern Cheyenne students drop out of Lame Deer as out of the other area high schools.[39]

An alterNative high school program has helped to improve the completion rates at Lame Deer High School Students now have opportunities to receive additional attention and individualized instruction Additionally, special initiatives to improve reading, math, and science instruction at all levels have contributed to a greater proportion of students moving toward proficient skill levels in math and science, as shown by the Montana Office of Instruction reports for 2005-06

Nevertheless, Northern Cheyenne students still have not performed as well as the Cheyenne educators feel they can One positive sign is the increasing numbers of high school graduates who enroll in college This indicates that student attitudes toward education are improving In 2005, half (50%) of St Labre students enrolled in college, 37% of Lame Deer High School graduates, and 35% of Northern Cheyenne Tribal School students enrolled in college Although this falls short of the 57% for all Montana high school graduates, the gap seems to be closing

RESERVATION INITIATIVES

Educators on the reservation are involved in many programs designed to increase the performance of students, beginning with the very youngest and including older students who need supplemental instruction Programs for middle school and high school students, such as Talent Search and Upward Bound, serve several local schools For more than 40 years, the Northern Cheyenne Tribe has obtained support for Head Start centers to provide early learning experiences for pre-school children The Northern Cheyenne Head Start program administers services to 3-5-year-old children of low-income families with a comprehensive program to meet their emotional, social, health, nutritional, and psychological needs

In addition a disability program is provided for children aged newborn to five years With seven centers across the reservation, Northern Cheyenne pre-schoolers develop the skills that help to prepare them for school Additionally, many Head Start centers incorporate Cheyenne language and culture into their programs Chief Dull Knife College partners with the Northern Cheyenne Head Start program to help Head Start teaching staff complete an associate degree in early childhood education For the last eight years, Lame Deer Public School has participated in GEAR UP (Gaining Early Awareness and Readiness for Undergraduate Programs) This provides tutoring, computer access, and a wide range of enrichment activities during the school year and in the summer.[40]

GEAR UP also provides services to parents, such as access to computers, workshops, and training GEAR UP works closely with other programs such as

Talent Search as well as the new Upward Bound program at Chief Dull Knife College to help Northern Cheyenne students complete high school successfully and prepare for entering college. The tribal college faculty members work closely with Lame Deer High School to offer courses for which students can receive credit following graduation and enrollment at the tribal college. Other cooperative efforts include developing a new math curriculum that can better prepare students for college level math.

Lame Deer Schools coordinate with the Northern Cheyenne Boys and Girls Club in Lame Deer to offer a safe place for students to go after school where they can receive academic help as well as recreational and other learning opportunities. When the Boys and Girls Club of the Northern Cheyenne Nation was formed in 1993, it was only the third Boys and Girls Club ever to be established on an American Indian reservation. Its mission is to promote healthy lifestyles and leadership for social, educational, vocational, cultural, and character development.

The Boys and Girls Club occupies a 15,000 square-foot building formerly donated to the Northern Cheyenne Tribe by the St. Labre Indian School Association. The building includes a gymnasium, classrooms and meeting rooms, offices, and kitchen facilities. This is one of two centers the club operates, one in Lame Deer and another in Ashland. The total membership in both clubs is 700 children. Lame Deer serves an average of 100 children per day, while Ashland serves 35.

Cheyenne children are among the most critically at-risk group in the United States for exposure to methamphetamine abuse. The club recently started a METHSmart program, which teaches the risks and consequences of using the drug. In July of 2000, then-Attorney General Janet Reno visited the club in Lame Deer to recognize its excellence and effectiveness. She directed the Department of Justice to provide seed money for this and other programs like it. Educators on the reservation have formed an informal group to address their common concerns. The Circle of Schools includes Lame Deer Elementary and High Schools, Colstrip Elementary and High Schools, St. Labre Indian Elementary and High Schools, Northern Cheyenne Tribal Elementary and High Schools, Ashland (elementary) Public School, the GEAR-UP initiative, the Northern Cheyenne Head Start Program, and Chief Dull Knife College. This Circle is an outgrowth of the statewide P-20 movement that gained popularity in about 2003. It was gaining a foothold on the Northern Cheyenne Reservation until an ill-conceived movement to establish a Northern Cheyenne Board of Regents was launched. After two years, the tribal council stopped this effort, and the tribal president said that any future efforts would be headed by Chief Dull Knife College.

Consequently, the Circle re-formed and has been meeting regularly at various venues. Chief Dull Knife College's involvement in this Circle stems from statistics showing the kind of students who were enrolling at Chief Dull Knife College and at other institutions of higher learning The over-all goal of the Circle of Schools is to systematize educational approaches from all of the diverse schools who serve Northern Cheyenne students and other area students who come to college The Circle aims to plug the achievement gaps in all academic areas but especially in math, science, and communications (English) The intentions are to remain non-political and to focus on bettering the educational opportunities of all of the students on or near the reservation

Conclusion

As the information presented shows, the Northern Cheyenne Nation's education institutions have made remarkable progress in the last several decades in trying to fulfill the goals and dreams of leaders like Chief Dull Knife and Dr John Woodenlegs Today, the tribe's education department supports these improvements by continuing to monitor the dropout and school completion rates of Cheyenne students This department also works with high school graduates to access tribal scholarships and other funding sources to support their college goals

Northern Cheyenne educators from all four local school districts and the tribal college communicate with one another to address issues that arise Despite the continuing needs to improve academic skills at the K-12 levels and to lower high school dropout rates, there is also good evidence that schooling is improving for the Northern Cheyenne

The fact that Chief Dull Knife College enrollment almost doubled between 2001 and 2005 shows that more students are looking to local schools to help them prepare for their futures Now with more resources in place to support higher achievement, Cheyenne educators are optimistic that more Northern Cheyenne students will graduate from high school and will continue to enter college and receive college degrees than ever before [41]

1 Ted Risingsun, who was a board member for Chief Dull Knife College, often quoted Chief Dull Knife's statement

2 John Woodenlegs was tribal president from 1955 until 1968 and had an honorary doctorate from Montana State University The library at Chief Dull Knife College is named in his honor

3 Bureau of the Census Census 2000 Summary File 3 (SF 3)

4 Ward, C , & Wilson, D (1989) Northern Cheyenne educational household census Report to the Northern Cheyenne Tribe, Lame Deer, MT

5 Ward & Wilson, Northern Cheyenne educational household census

6 Snipp, M (1989) American Indians The First of this Land NY Russell Sage Foundation

7 T Risingsun (personal communication), 1989

8 Rowland F (1994) Tribal education A case study of Northern Cheyenne elders (Doctoral dissertation, Montana State University) Baird-Olson K & Ward, C (2000) Recovery and resistance The renewal of traditional spirituality among Native American women American Indian Culture and Research Journal 2 1(4) 1 35

9 Bryan, W L , & Yellowtail, W P (1985) Future high school education options for the Northern Cheyenne Tribe An education planning and strategy study Report prepared for the Northern Cheyenne Tribe Bozeman, MT Bureau of Indian Affairs, Office of Indian Education Programs U S Department of the Interior

10 Bryan & Yellowtail Future high school education options for the Northern Cheyenne Tribe

11 Stark, M (2005, April 10) Giving and getting at St Labre School Northern Cheyenne sue for share of mission's wealth *The Billings Gazette* Retrieved from website http //billingsgazette net/articles/2005/04/10/state/export/201984 txt

12 St Labre Indian Mission (2007) *Keeping the Miracle Alive* [Brochure] Ashland, MT

13 Stark, Giving and getting at St Labre School

14 Stark, Giving and getting at St Labre School

15 Stark, Giving and getting at St Labre School

16 R Little Bear (personal communication) Dec 2007

17 Bryan & Yellowtail, Future high school education options for the Northern Cheyenne Tribe

18 Rosenfelt, D M (1973, April) Indian schools and community control *Stanford Law Review 25*(4), 489-550

19 Rosenfelt said in his report that no graduate of Busby was known to have completed college in its 50 year existence However, this is not true Little Bear's sister, Dolores Little Bear Hart, graduated from the school in Busby (then called the Tongue River Boarding School) in 1952 She went on to become a registered nurse and eventually a nurse practitioner Although their freshmen class at the Tongue River Boarding School was large, by graduation time there were only two left in their class—her and Elizabeth White Fox Hart, D (personal communication), Jan 8, 2008

20 Footnotes from the original Letter from Arthur L MacDonald, Ph D and William D Bliss, Ph D , to Edward M Kennedy, Jan 7, 1969, in SENATE COMM ON LABOR AND PUBLIC WELFARE, THE EDUCATION OF AMERICAN INDIANS A COMPEN-DIUM OF FEDERAL BOARDING SCHOOL EVALUATIONS, 84S (1969) OUR BROTHER'S KEEPER THE INDIAN IN WHITE AMERICA 40 (E Cahn ed 1970)

21 Footnotes from the original Officials from the BIA agency on the reservation and the Area Office in Billings, MT, suggested that the school become part of the public school system, but the community preferred to operate the school with funds obtained through contract with the BIA T Risingsun, chairman of Busby School Board, Busby MT (personal communication) Nov 22, 1971

22 Northern Cheyenne Follow Through Program proposal (1980), p 8 Submitted to the U S Department of Education Lame Deer, MT

23 Crawford, J The special case of bilingual education for Indian students *Education Week 6*(16) 44

24 Bryan & Yellowtail, Future high school education options for the Northern Cheyenne Tribe

25 Bryan & Yellowtail Future high school education options for the Northern Cheyenne Tribe

26 Ward C (2005) *Native Americans in the school system family, community, and academic achievement* Lanham, MD AltaMira Press

27 Bryan & Yellowtail, Future high school education options for the Northern Cheyenne Tribe

28 Bryan & Yellowtail Future high school education options for the Northern Cheyenne Tribe

29 Lame Deer Schools website http //www lamedeer k12 mt us phtemp com/aboutus htm

30 Ward, *Native Americans in the school system*

31 Ward, C (1990) Northern Cheyenne Dropout Study report, 1990

32 Colstrip currently offers classes in Native Studies and teaches a Northern Cheyenne language, reading, and writing program via satellite from Chief Dull Knife College

33 Jamison, M , Getting the big picture Gail Small, Northern Cheyenne Reservation Retrieved Dec 11, 2007, from http //www missoulian com/specials/northernlights/nchevenne html

34 G Small (personal communication), Dec 21, 2007 *Native Action 20th Anniversary Report, 1984-2007* (2008) Lame Deer, MT, Native Action

35 Clifford A (1993) Northern Cheyenne struggle for high school after 30 years *Indian Country Today 13*(8) p A1

36 Ward, *Native Americans in the school system*

37 Ward, C & Widdison-Jones K (2007) Evaluation of the Northern Cheyenne RSI program

38 Ward, C & Wilson D , (1985) Northern Cheyenne adult education survey Report to Dull Knife Memorial College, Lame Deer, MT

39 http //www opi mt gov/measurement/Index html

40 Lame Deer High School website http //www lamedeer k12 mt us phtemp com/GetrUp htm

41 Ward, C & Widdison-Jones, K , (2006) Title III Evaluation Report 2005-06 Chief Dull Knife College

Chief Dull Knife College

IN 1878, CHIEF Dull Knife said to his Cheyenne people, "We can no longer live the way we used to There is a new way of life that we are going to know Let us ask for schools, that way our children can attend them and learn this new way of life "[1]

At the time, some of his people called him "the wife of a white man ' according-ing to Ted Rising Sun, a charge of treason at the time Dull Knife knew as well as anyone the danger of empowering the white man Yet he also recognized that education was essential for his people to survive and adapt to the changing times He believed in adaptation, not assimilation However, from the 1880s until the 1970s the only educational options were schools designed to assimilate students into the mainstream

From the time of the first English settlements, American Indians have been encouraged to participate in the rituals of Western civilization The goal has sel-dom been enhancing the Indian students or the well being of their tribes Educa-tion based on assimilation has never worked with the Northern Cheyenne people and others in similar circumstances, and these policies have had a residual negative effect

When the Northern Cheyennes sent their best and brightest students away to attend college, many dropped out and returned Their parents and the com-munity knew they were good children and smart Why did so few graduate? There were many reasons Young people on the Northern Cheyenne Reservation and other reservations grow up in culturally distinct communities Despite struggles with poverty, substance abuse, unemployment, and political disenfranchisement, the Northern Cheyennes and others have retained many distinctive cultural tradi-tions The students were not prepared for the hostility they often encountered in larger academic institutions—school officials and classmates who believed in stereotypes of American Indians as "dirty " "lazy," "drunk," and "dumb "

Student of the Year, 2005–2006

Mariah Maxwell was selected to be the college's American Indian College Fund Student of the Year for the 2005–2006 academic year. Maxwell is a member of the Northern Cheyenne Tribe. It was a struggle for her to attend college because she has six small children, but because of her determination and dedication to her studies, Maxwell was on the CDKC President's List three times. She was a member of the American Indian Business Leaders Club for two years, including one year as president. She graduated from Chief Dull Knife College in 2006 and went to Montana State University-Billings. After she receives her Bachelor's Degree in Elementary Education, she plans to get her Master's Degree in Administration. (Photo by Kathleen Beartusk)

Student of the Year, 2006–2007

Chief Dull Knife College selected Tommy B. Robinson to be the American Indian College Fund Student of the Year for the 2006–2007 academic year. Robinson is an enrolled member of the Crow Tribe, but he is part Northern Cheyenne and has lived on the Northern Cheyenne Reservation all his life. When he was in high school, he took out a loan that was just for the youth and started his own business raising cattle. While attending Chief Dull Knife College, he was the student senate president for one year and a member of the American Indian Science and Engineering Society (AISES) Chapter. He made the CDKC President's List four times and the National Dean's List two times. Robinson graduated from Chief Dull Knife College in 2007 and went to Oral Roberts University in Tulsa, OK. He is majoring in biology with a concentration on health professions. After graduating from Oral Roberts University, he plans to attend the University of Montana and get his Doctorate Degree in Physical Therapy. (Photo by Kathleen Beartusk)

Unlike many of their relatively care-free classmates, the college students from the reservations often were responsible for children of their own or for caring for elderly family members The nearest community colleges and four-year institutions were at least 110 miles from their extended family and cultural support systems on the Northern Cheyenne Reservation

Nor were they prepared for the academic rigor they encountered at the larger academic institutions Colleges and universities across the country struggle with high school graduates who are under prepared for college work [2] Northern Cheyenne students also lack American Indian role models and sometimes face under-prepared and/or unqualified K-12 teachers, inadequate school materials and equipment, and apathetic parental attitudes toward education

It therefore became obvious to a group of American Indian educators that a successful educational program must create higher education institutions that could provide learning experiences related to the students, their culture, and their environment In 1968 the first tribal college opened its doors on the Navajo Reservation in the Southwest This group of educators promoted the idea of creating colleges on their own reservations, and although initially opposed by the Bureau of Indian Affairs (BIA), the tribal colleges and universities movement was born and continues to thrive today As word spread across the Northern Plains, tribes started colleges in North Dakota, South Dakota, and Montana

HISTORY OF THE COLLEGE

Chief Dull Knife College, originally known as Dull Knife Memorial College, began as a vocational training program, housed in Army tents, in Ashland, MT, in 1972 The original curriculum reflected the West's coal boom during the 1970s—training Northern Cheyennes for mining and construction jobs as well as forestry

The program continued to operate out of make-shift facilities until 1975, when the Northern Cheyenne Tribe received funding from the Indian Technical Assistance Center of the Bureau of Indian Affairs for construction and operation of the Northern Cheyenne Indian Action Program, Inc

The tribe chartered the Indian Action Program in September 1975 by Tribal Ordinance 5(76) Tribal leaders, program staff, and the board of trustees soon recognized the need for additional vocational programs, as well as general education and liberal arts The first academic courses were offered in the winter of 1978 as a satellite campus of Miles Community College

During that quarter, a naming contest for the new tribal college was held, and Tim Wilson, a member of the Northern Cheyenne tribe who ultimately became a medical doctor, submitted the name Dull Knife Memorial College Northern Cheyenne Tribal Council Ordinance 5(79) subsequently changed the name and authorized the college to award degrees Although the academic curriculum from

1978-1979 was limited, the vocational curriculum grew to include wastewater disposal and surveying. The relationship with Miles Community College continued through Fall Quarter 1979, when Dull Knife Memorial College was given accreditation candidacy status by the Northwest Association of Schools and Colleges.

From 1979 to 1984, the college expanded its curricular offerings and also offered a wide variety of student activities including Region IX intercollegiate men and women's basketball teams. In 1985, Northern Cheyenne Tribal Council Ordinance 8(85) chartered Dull Knife Memorial College, granting autonomy to the college and revising the charter to provide for an elected rather than an appointed board. To extend the benefits of a tribally controlled college to other reservations in the state, the Northern Cheyenne college became the sponsoring institution for both Fort Belknap College and Stone Child College. The Northwest Commission on Colleges and Universities granted full accreditation to Chief Dull Knife College in 1995.

In 2001, the name of the college was changed to Chief Dull Knife College (CDKC) to emphasize the importance of Dull Knife as a chief of the Northern Cheyenne people. (Dull Knife is a Sioux name, but among the Northern Cheyenne, he is known as *Vooheheva* or Morning Star.)

In 2007 Chief Dull Knife College was one of 36 tribal colleges and universities in the United States, including seven within Montana—the most in any state. The curriculum has expanded to provide the Northern Cheyenne people and their neighbors with access to a variety of programs leading to the degrees of Associate of Arts, Associate of Applied Science, and certificates in several skill areas.

The two-year institution is accredited by the Northwest Commission on Colleges and Universities. It is a community-based, tribally controlled college and land-grant institution. Its open-admission policy provides a standing invitation to Cheyennes and their neighbors in the region into the world of career and liberal arts education.

Goals of the college include the following:

1 To be financially stable and self-sufficient.

2 To provide educational resources and experiences to assist community members in acquiring improved skills for work and life.

3 To maintain an accredited institution of higher education on the Northern Cheyenne Indian Reservation capable of providing college transfer programs and vocational skills training to increase the educational level and meet the training needs of the students and the community.

4 To provide effective support services to students that will facilitate their successful completion of programs offered by the college.

5 To provide a language program to preserve, teach, research and support traditional Cheyenne culture, language, and history.

CULTURAL MISSION

Throughout its more than 30-year history, the college has provided a cultural foundation for its students while also helping them prepare for a changing world. Almost 42% of the reservation's people were under the age of 18, and another 50% were between the ages of 18 and 64 in the 2000 Census.[3] With this high proportion of young people, it follows that young Northern Cheyenne can find fewer and fewer elders, who are the keepers of Cheyenne knowledge, to learn from.

Research on the reservation has shown that knowledge of the Cheyenne ways is correlated with educational success.[4] The students must learn about their culture and their history not just to keep that knowledge alive. It also gives students the foundation they need to succeed in other endeavors. They have to know who they are and from where they came.

There is a healthy need in Indian country to "save" traditional American Indian cultures as an abstract, theoretical, and practical "good." After a century of military conquest, economic disenfranchisement, and political isolation, tribes need their traditional culture to be an active and critically important part of community survival in education, economic development, and social integrity. This, in turn, contributes to the community's ability to build a sustainable society.

The college fulfills its cultural mission in many ways. Like other tribal colleges, CDKC maintains a cultural heritage center (the Florence Whiteman Cultural Center) that sponsors programs in Cheyenne language, history and culture from the Cheyenne perspective.[5] Programs from this center sponsor language immersion camps and Native American Week every September. Community members participate with tribal college students and staff in a variety of activities, such as a bow and arrow shoot, a tipi-raising class and contest, a "handgame" tournament, and cultural mini-courses that demonstrate cutting dry meat, making frybread, and flint-knapping arrowheads. The college also certifies Cheyenne language teachers, as discussed in the language chapter of this book.

In 2007, student Roman Fisher, 28, talked to a magazine reporter about the importance of Chief Dull Knife College. Fisher is an eighth generation traditional singer and drummer. His family taught him songs, and he hopes to pass these traditions on to others.

> There are so many Native Americans who think that high school is the last
> days of their education, and they go on to drink alcohol and do drugs. The
> reason why I'm here is a lot high school students are raised on MTV or TV and
> becoming acculturated just by watching all that rap. They are starting to lose
> focus of their own ways like singing, traditional dancing, and the language. I
> have younger cousins who speak kind of Black, like how they do on TV. That's
> pretty weird to me growing up in a traditional family."

The Cheyenne have encountered so much oppression. It's hard to get back to where we were The people my age need to get back to that way of thinking, that knowledge of our traditional ways That's important because there are so many tribes that have lost their way of life, their language, their land, and their identities They are being acculturated into the modern ways [6]

Tribal colleges, such as CDKC, were originally established to provide educational programs in a culturally appropriate environment for students such as Fisher and for others who may not know as much about their origins However, it has been difficult for the colleges to find funds for cultural programs The funding formulas for tribal colleges ordinarily support only the most bare-bones student services and instruction Tribal colleges can support activities directly related to only the most elementary functions of the institution, such as teaching mathematics or English and keeping student records

Thus cultural projects, which formed the rationale for establishing tribal colleges, often go unfunded For example, CDKC in recent years had to reassign the Dean of Cultural Affairs position as part of the duties of the present president of the college CDKC has received some funding in the cultural area, getting a grant from the Administration for Native Americans to teach fluent Cheyenne speakers to read, write, and develop Cheyenne language curriculum The center also received funding from the state of Montana under the Office of the Governor's Tribal Histories and Equipment Initiative, an initiative that made this history book possible

SERVING COMMUNITY NEEDS

It has been said that tribal colleges and universities are under-funded miracles [7] CDKC definitely fits that description Despite financial limitations and the challenges of serving this community, it has succeeded in increasing student enrollment, increasing student retention, increasing numbers of students realizing their educational goals, and expanding programs and services to the community

CDKC, like other schools on the reservation, must address the needs of a community characterized by persistent low educational achievement, poverty, unemployment, and underemployment across several generations The tribal college was created to serve the Northern Cheyenne people, but it also serves students from surrounding communities, many of whom share the obstacles that the Indian students face Of the 300 students each academic year, approximately 85% of these students are American Indian, 70% are female, and a significant number of the students are either heads of households or are un-married, primary caregivers to young children In addition, 90% of entering students are low-income, and 80% are first generation college students [8] Some of the students have disabilities

When one considers the social milieu that they were raised in, it is not surprising that 90% of the students are eligible for federal student financial aid assistance, and 80% are fully eligible for Pell Grants. According to the 2000 census, nearly 50% of Cheyenne families live under the poverty level, and unemployment fluctuated from 60-85% because jobs are scarce and often seasonal on the Northern Cheyenne Reservation.[5] Clearly, without the opportunity to attend Chief Dull Knife College, most of these students would not have had the opportunity to pursue and realize their post-secondary educational goals.

In 2007, one student described the importance of the tribal college to expand his circle of support to succeed. Perry Big Left Hand, 28, left the reservation to join the Army. He came back after six years of active duty and two tours in Iraq with a traumatic brain injury. "When I was away in the Army, people asked me

Chief Dull Knife College serves the Northern Cheyenne community and their neighbors, providing a foundation in the tribe's history and traditions while preparing students for the future. Pictured are (left to right) John J. Wooden Legs, president of the board of directors and Vietnam veteran; Ronelle Renee Beartusk, a student and a sixth generation descendant of Chief Dull Knife; and Sgt. Perry Big Left Hand, a student who served for six years in the U.S. Army. (Photo by Kathleen Beartusk)

where I was from, and I would tell them Lame Deer, MT They would ask me what kind of Indian I was, and I would tell them I was Northern Cheyenne Having a strong identity is important because it gives people something to look forward to It helps prove people wrong about a certain identity, whether that is American Indian or whether someone is disabled," he said

Some people told him he wouldn't be able to do much after his brain injury, but he was determined Attending Chief Dull Knife College helps him be more active in his tribal culture and learn more about the history of his people 'People should be proud to be Northern Cheyenne It defines my identity, being a survivor I can help other people and show them what I did to overcome such obstacles "[10]

Nearly 60% of all Chief Dull Knife College's graduates transition to a four-year college or university To make it possible for these students to continue their studies, the college has established and maintains articulation agreements with institutions within the Montana University System that facilitate "seamless" transfer and acceptance of all credits and degrees earned at CDKC

The college also makes it possible for community members to earn bachelor's and master's degrees on-line primarily from Rocky Mountain College, a private four-year college located in Billings In 2007, the college also had three staff members enrolled in an on-line MBA program through Gonzaga University For the most part, students taking these degree completion courses were community members working within a local school system or tribal program However, three CDKC staff members completed bachelor's degrees and one a master's degree through the Rocky Mountain College on-line program In 2007 an employee at the Bureau of Indian Affairs, two employees at St Labre Indian School, the CDKC Student Activities Director, and one Northern Cheyenne Headstart employee were enrolled in advanced courses

STUDENT SUCCESS

CDKC is changing the poverty and unemployment levels, one graduate at a time The graduates have been employed in a wide range of both general labor and professional positions Many of the vocational students in the areas of carpentry, welding, heavy equipment operation, and secretarial science held positions both on and off the reservation Most vocational graduates were employed with the Montana Power Company (PPI Montana) and had maintained that employment for over 20 years They worked as utility men, plant apprentices, boilermakers, and office personnel with PPI In 2007, one female graduate was the administrative assistant to the company president and therefore involved with management, while another was involved with the company's personnel department Other vocational graduates had started their own construction businesses, found employment with tribal agencies such as Northern Cheyenne Housing Authority and Northern Cheyenne Utilities, or returned to college to pursue a transfer curriculum

Graduates of the Associate in Arts degree programs had also found employment in a wide range of positions. The immediate past academic dean at CDKC (Judith Davis) was a graduate of the college after completing her bachelor's degree and master's degree and returning to the college. A student who graduated with an emphasis in business (Jerry Fozzard) started his own international medical placement service headquartered in Illinois and provides placement opportunities for doctors and nurses throughout the world

Other associate degree graduates went on to complete teaching and/or counseling degrees (Janice Breyer, Jewel Davenport, Robert Shotgunn, Alvera Cook, John Currier) and were employed in local school systems both on and off the reservation. In 2007, the president of the Northern Cheyenne Tribe (Eugene Little Coyote) was also a graduate of Chief Dull Knife College as were several tribal employees. The college recruited several of its own graduates who went on to complete bachelor's and master's degrees (Michelle Spang, Rae Peppers, Verda King, Debra Reed, Michelle Curlee)

The dean of students at the college (Zane Spang) in 2007 was a CDKC graduate as were the Upward Board Program director (Evelyn Roundstone) and counselor (Delores Shoulderblade) and the college's bookstore director (Michelle Threefingers) CDKC alumni also filled part-time faculty, secretarial positions, administrative assistant positions, maintenance positions, and various student activity positions at the college

The success of these graduates resulted from several CDKC initiatives, as well as their own hard work. CDKC expanded its science curriculum to include the courses needed by students who would like to pursue science and technology or health fields as majors in their bachelor's and graduate degrees

The tribal college increased the number and range of opportunities for college students to participate in internships that helped prepare them for successful transitions to four-year programs. Over the last several years more than two dozen students participated in internships either on the CDKC campus in science, math, and technology, or on the campuses of the University of Montana in Missoula and Montana State University-Bozeman. These experiences helped students feel better prepared to pursue bachelor's and graduate degrees after they graduate from CDKC [1]

CDKC was a major participant in the National Science Foundation's Tribal College University Partnership (TCUP), through which it enhanced math and science teaching through innovative pedagogy and rigorous evaluation. It developed and expanded science programs with a grant from the National Science

Dr. Alonzo Spang graduated from Colstrip High School in 1953 as class valedictorian. He went on to earn a doctorate in education and became the first American Indian (and Northern Cheyenne) agency superintendent of the Northern Cheyenne Reservation. After a distinguished career with the BIA, Spang became president of Dull Knife Memorial College in 1994. (Photo by Kathleen Beartusk)

Foundation's Rural Systemic Initiative (RSI) program. It developed innovative and effective techniques in learning skills and established learning labs to assist students with self-paced software programs in math courses.

The USDA Extension program at the college expanded it services to the reservation community and offered a variety of financial workshops, tax preparation, and nutrition programs designed to target community needs.

The tribal college has stretched the horizons of reservation residents, some of whom never previously considered a trip outside of Montana. At the same time, cultural exchanges and internships may have helped dispel stereotypes by everyone involved. For example, three faculty members and several students participated in cultural exchanges in Mali over three years In Africa, they worked with farmers and Peace Corps volunteers to deliver Integrated Pest Management information, helping Malian farmers learn about how to combat the cowpea pest problem [12]

CDKC students successfully interned at Brown University, the University of Montana and Montana State University in "Bridges" programs Although most of these internships were science related, it gave participating students an opportunity to experience other cultures and communities

WORK WITH OTHER SCHOOLS

The drop-out rates on the Northern Cheyenne Reservation are high and the college preparation is poor, as discussed in the preceding chapter Therefore, CDKC has felt compelled to help improve schooling for Northern Cheyenne students by coordinating with and supporting pre-K-12 schools that serve the Northern Cheyenne Reservation As mentioned in an earlier chapter, this has included working closely with Lame Deer High School to offer college level courses for students planning to enroll at CDKC Other initiatives include providing math and science instruction and technical assistance to math and science teachers at the elementary and middle school levels

CDKC received support from the National Science Foundation through its Rural Systemic Initiative (RSI) to develop math and science courses for local teachers that helped them master the material they needed to improve their classroom instruction This project, which was very successful in attracting teachers from all of the local schools, contributed to improvements in math and science skill levels among Northern Cheyenne students Another National Science Foundation project, funded though the Tribal College and University Partnership (TCUP) program, provided the resources to improve CDKC curriculum in both math and science In 2007, the positive impact of this project was starting to show in students' increased success and higher performance in math and science [13]

With the experience gained in these programs, CDKC began reaching out to the Lame Deer High School, where many CDKC students graduated, to work on improving math and science preparation at the secondary levels This effort was also coordinating with the new Upward Bound program that CDKC was awarded in 2007, which serves students at St Labre Indian School, Lame Deer High School, and Northern Cheyenne Tribal School

LIMITS ON FACILITIES AND STAFFING

When the U S Congress enacted the Tribal College or University Assistance Act in 1978, it authorized $5,820 per pupil to serve as the baseline institutional funding at each college This amount has never been appropriated, however The tribal colleges have had to operate with as little as $2,800 per ISC (Indian Student Count), up more recently to $4,200 per ISC, far below actual costs per student [1]

This federal funding is based upon the number of Indian students at each tribal college About 15% of the CDKC students are not covered by the federal funding In Montana, the state provides some funds to the tribal colleges for educating such non-Indian students, who are referred to as non-beneficiary students Each year the presidents of the seven Montana tribal colleges have to implore the appropriate state legislative committee to appropriate funding for these students Even when the Montana Legislature approves funding, it is typically only $1,500 per student This means that CDKC supplements the state of Montana approximately $4,000 per non-beneficiary student yearly

In short, Chief Dull Knife College must depend largely upon special funding to launch new academic programs or services CDKC has demonstrated steady but meager growth over the years in a fiscal sense, but it has not kept up with the expanding student population Between 2002 and 2007, CDKC increased its student headcount by 10% per year and the full-time student enrollment by 20% each year The lack of funding for staff has severely limited the college's ability to provide essential programs With more students, the college needs additional classrooms, library and archival space, laboratories, and student recreational facilities

In order to sustain the most basic operations required to meet accreditation standards and institutional effectiveness, the college had to cut two faculty positions, the dean of cultural affairs, finance manager, an archivist within the library and culture studies area three facility maintenance positions, and the institutional development position With these necessary reductions in staff, the remaining staff had to assume additional responsibilities, making it impossible for the college to add programs and services with existing staff The success being realized with increased student enrollment and the identified need for expanded programs and services has seriously been impacted by reductions in funding

Like most tribal colleges, Chief Dull Knife College was born in meager facilities—Army tents in Ashland MT, and operated there for three years until a small building (12,000 square feet) was built in Lame Deer using funding from the Indian Technical Assistance Center of the Bureau of Indian Affairs The original facility was constructed primarily for vocational training purposes In subsequent years, construction grants from the National Science Foundation, USDA, and the American Indian College Fund/Lily Foundation have allowed the college to remodel the facility It currently houses laboratories and classrooms for science, math, computer science, agriculture, and secretarial science courses, as well as the college's extension program The facilities heating system was also converted from coal-fired boilers to propane heat While an electrical retrofit was completed as well expanded technology in the classrooms and labs created additional electrical complications

In 1979, the college acquired a facility for the college library it was originally constructed for the tribal commodity distribution program, and building trades students remodeled it An adjacent building, built to house an inpatient drug and alcohol program, was given to the college in 1980 With the assistance of renovation grants, the college's building trades students remodeled the facility which houses four classrooms, faculty and staff offices the college cafeteria, bookstore, a student learning lab, and the college administration offices Many students have children The college remodeled an old BIA mechanical shop to make a day care center Later it was converted to a student activity center

Unfortunately, these remodeled buildings were not originally created as college facilities so their designs are less than ideal and they are not energy efficient Records indicate an average of 390 hours of instructional use per year in a facility designed for 270 hours The largest room on campus for classes and/or community meetings is 1,200 square feet, which prevents the college from hosting workshops seminars, classes, and meetings for more than 60 people

By working creatively with many different agencies and nonprofit organizations, CDKC has been able to build some new facilities on campus and make some older ones more efficient The new buildings are the Early Childhood Learning Center funded by HUD and USDA the adult education/literacy center funded by the Lily Foundation and USDA the vocational skills center funded by USDA the Florence Whiteman Culture Center funded by the Lily Foundation and a recently completed visiting lecturer center funded by USDA

All of these facilities were designed and constructed utilizing sustainable green-build technology in cooperation with the American Indian Housing Initiative This is a national collaboration in public scholarship joining Penn State University the University of Washington the University of Wisconsin and Chief Dull Knife College The initiative demonstrates green building technologies and sustainable development strategies The straw-bale buildings have resulted in lowered utility costs to the college

Nevertheless as CDKC grows it will need additional land for the campus and construction funds The most immediate needs are for a new classroom/office complex a student multipurpose center a new library and a new maintenance facility

Conclusion

Chief Dull Knife College and other tribal colleges and universities provide a cultural education as well as a more standard academic education to American Indian students Through education the Cheyennes can adapt to the changing world, as Chief Dull Knife wanted them to do They can continue to develop their local economy and tribal government and preserve Indian rights to land and resources With their cultural education the students can help to revitalize their language and culture Knowing more about who they are and where they come from fortifies the students for their roles in modern society, whether they continue their studies at other universities take positions in the private or public sector or create their own businesses

As student Roman Fisher told the *Tribal College Journal* A lot of people my age are just now beginning to understand that we are losing our culture and language Having our own history our own secrets our own songs, stories of how we came to be—that's what separates us from the rest of the world because we know where we come from "

1 T Risingsun was a board member for the tribal college who often quoted Chief Dull Knife's statement

2 Alliance for Excellent Education 2006) *Paying double Inadequate high schools and community college remediation* Washington DC Alliance for Excellent Education 2006 Retrieved December 2007 from http www all ed org files archive publications remediation pdf

3 Bureau of the Census Census 2000 Summary File 3 (SF 3

4 Ward C J (2005 *Native Americans in the school system Family community, and academic achievement* Walnut Creek CA AltaMira Press

5 Simonelli R (2003) Keeping it alive Centers contribute to cultural renaissance on college campuses *Tribal College Journal* 14(2) Winter 2003

6 Braun J 2008 What's in a name? Tribal colleges nourish students cultural identity *Tribal College Journal* 19(3) Spring 2008

7 Houser S 1991) *Underfunded miracles Tribal colleges* Washington DC Department of Education Indian Nations at Risk Task Force 1991 Available online in full text from ERIC 337 2 http www eric ed gov

8 Enrollment student financial aid matriculation and retention data from Chief Dull Knife College files

9 Bureau of the Census Census 2000 Summary File 3 (SF 3)

10 Braun (2008)

11 Ward C & Widdison-Jones K (2006 *Title III Evaluation Report 2005-06* Report to CDKC

12 CDKC research reaches from Mali to Lame Deer *Tribal College Journal* 16 2 Winter 2004

13 Madsen B Hodgson T & Ward C 2006 Pathways to success in pre-college mathematics *Tribal College Journal* 18 2 Winter 2006

14 *Tribal colleges An introduction* Alexandria VA American Indian Higher Education Consortium n d available at http www aihec org documents Research intro pdf

Energy Development on the
Northern Cheyenne Reservation

We can no longer live the way we used to There is a new way of life that we
are going to know

Chief Dull Knife,
1878[1]

LITTLE DID CHIEF Dull Knife know in 1878 what that "new way of life"
would be like for his people Less than a century later, the Northern Cheyennes, who had lived for centuries as part of the land and as stewards of
Mother Earth, would be asked to rip their Mother apart to mine coal And if they
wouldn't, others—newcomers to Cheyenne country—would

In the early 1920s the Northern Pacific Railroad was looking for land in
eastern Montana Its mine at Red Lodge was not producing enough coal to fuel
railroad's locomotives More than that, the men who mined the coal had become
increasingly prone to strike Geological surveys of the Rosebud country in 1913
and 1915 had found a significant field of sub-bituminous coal After some corporate soul searching, the railroad decided to shift its coal-supply production facility
from Red Lodge to a new coal camp called Colstrip in 1923 [2] (It should have been
"Coalstrip," but an error in the Post Office's administration in Washington left the
tiny village with its name misspelled forever [3]) No one could have predicted at the
time the impact that the discovery of coal and its development at Colstrip would
have on the Northern Cheyenne Reservation, 20 miles away

Northern Pacific hired a construction contractor, Foley Brothers of Minne-
sota, to operate its new coal mine They originally planned to use steam shovels to
remove the "overburden" (the layer of earth above the seams of coal) and scoop out
the coal An enormous amount of reasonably clean water would have been needed
to make the steam for the shovels, and the Foley engineers quickly learned that
the water in the Colstrip area was heavily alkaline, which would have seriously
corroded the expensive machinery The only alternative lay in electric power [4]

It just so happened that in 1924 a utility company in Montana was available to provide that electric power to the Colstrip coal mining camp It was the
Montana Power Company The Montana Power Company grew out of a great

dish of corporate spaghetti cooked up during the beginning of the 20th century Big business in Montana grew under the direction of John D Ryan, whose aptitude for business allies and mineral alloys alike brought the properties of the old copper kings together as the Anaconda Copper Mining Company in 1915 At one time this collection of businesses owned all but one of the state's newspapers and accounted for three-fourths of Montana's payroll Some authors said that a significant portion of their money went to the state's legislature [5]

To Anaconda, Ryan added the Montana Power Company in 1912 Collectively called simply The Company, the Anaconda Copper Mining Company and the Montana Power Company ruled the region Anaconda owed its success partly to Ryan's vision of a technologically cutting-edge mining operation, which in the early 20th century meant the electrification of its mines [6]

In 1924, Montana Power built a 100-mile transmission line from Billings to Colstrip, enabling Foley Brothers to open its first pit with what was at the time the largest mechanical shovel ever built Colstrip became the first open-pit coal mine in the United States to be completely electrified [7]

Energy development brought a few opportunities to the Northern Cheyennes from the 1920s through the '50s, but it also brought problems A few Cheyennes worked occasionally in the Foley mines in Colstrip, where they camped during the work week near cliffs inhabited by a spirit they called the Yellow Painted Man The Yellow Painted Man visited them in their camp, providing them with spiritual comfort while they worked almost as migrants 20 miles from their home When the cliffs crumbled before the rugged power of a dragline, the Yellow Painted Man vanished with them No Cheyenne has seen him since, and afterward the Cheyennes refused to work for the Foleys [8]

WALLOWING BULL V TERMINATION

In the 1940s, energy companies realized that the Northern Cheyenne Reservation had some of the region's richest fossil fuel resources In 1948, two energy promoters, Martin Naddy and A E Beeler, convinced Tribal President John Russell that if the tribe were to petition the Secretary of the Interior to terminate (end its status as a federally-recognized Indian tribe), there would be a hefty payment to every Cheyenne man, woman, and child on the reservation They said that the potential oil revenues would make the Northern Cheyenne people rich [9]

The tribal government was young and inexperienced, having been created in its modern form only 13 years earlier under the federal Indian Reorganization Act The council passed a resolution requesting termination, which, fortunately, was denied by the Secretary of the Interior The next tribal chairman, Rufus Wallowing Bull understood that termination would mean the loss the Cheyennes' homeland

and dissolution of the Cheyenne as a tribe Their culture might crumble like the cliffs inhabited by Yellow Painted Man Wallowing Bull convinced his fellow tribal members that survival lay in the strength, not the dissolution, of the tribe

The Cheyennes were lucky If the Russell's administration had petitioned for termination in the 1950s instead of the 1940s, the Interior Secretary would have accepted their decision By then, termination was the federal policy In particular, Congress targeted the resource-rich tribes for termination Indeed many tribes became destitute after losing their tribal status [10]

However, the people elected Rufus Wallowing Bull in 1948, and he served until 1952 The writer Mari Sandoz once remarked that someday the Cheyennes would put up a statue of Rufus Wallowing Bull in Lame Deer [11] Historian Richard Drinnon called Wallowing Bull a "tribal patriot "[12]

RACE AND ENERGY

In the coal town of Colstrip, racism was as bad or worse than in other reservation border towns Aside from the handful of Cheyenne miners who worked there for a few years, the coal camp had only a few Bureau of Indian Affairs (BIA) employees, and some Cheyenne children attended Colstrip High School Dr Alonzo Spang graduated from Colstrip High School in 1953 as class valedictorian Spang went on to earn a doctorate in education and became the first Indian (and Northern Cheyenne) agency superintendent of the Northern Cheyenne Reservation After a distinguished career with the BIA, Spang became president of Dull Knife Memorial College (now known as Chief Dull Knife College) in 1994

Spang graduated from high school a year ahead of local rancher Wally McRae, who doesn't remember racism being a problem "When I went to school," remembers McRae "roughly half of the graduates came from the reservation The other half came from Colstrip I was in the middle I didn't come from either place But there were not two factions There was a cohesive community spanning between Lame Deer and Colstrip that held us together "[13]

Racial, cultural, economic, and community divisions often act with subtlety, not always with the glare of ethnic slurs, but with different, almost whispered, feelings on both sides Wholly different Colstrips emerge from each "One of the good things about being a youngster," explained Spang, ' is that you don't know that you're being discriminated against, so it doesn't hurt your psyche right then After, you reflect on things

"For instance, I was never invited to a home My brother and I and others, we were never invited to homes over there but other non-Indian students were invited to their homes in Colstrip People really didn't acknowledge you We were the darlings on the football field or on the basketball court or on the baseball

Since the 1920s, the town of Colstrip has had a symbiotic relationship with the Northern Cheyennes, mutually dependent but often antagonistic. (Photo by John Warner)

diamond, but once that final whistle blew, all that evaporated, and I was just another Cheyenne from the reservation."[14]

He certainly seemed to have been popular with his fellow students. Spang's high school classmates elected him as their delegate to Montana's Boys' State. When the principal submitted his name to the Women's Club, he was rejected. Go back and get another candidate, they told the principal. Another election—this time Spang won by a wider margin. The Women's Club relented and allowed Spang to go to Boys' State, so long as a non-Indian student would accompany him as a co-delegate.[15] Yet whatever new challenges the coal camp brought to the Northern Cheyennes, they were paltry compared to what happened next.

CHEYENNE COAL LEASES

In 1974, the Organization of Petroleum Exporting Countries (OPEC) declared an oil embargo against the United States. The "energy crisis" of the 1970s set in motion a frenzy of activity by states and corporate interests eager to find new sources of fuel. One of these new sources was coal. In 1976, Montana historian K. Ross Toole called the Northern Cheyenne "the most important Indian tribe in this country."[16] He described them as having taken "a page from the Shah of Iran" and quoted the tribal attorney calling the Cheyennes "the American Arabs."[17]

In late 1965, a consulting geologist made inquiries to the Bureau of Indian Affairs (BIA) superintendent of the Northern Cheyenne agency about obtaining a permit to explore the reservation for coal. The superintendent, charged with developing income-producing opportunities for the tribal government and individual Cheyennes, "responded enthusiastically."[18] More than half the people on the reservation were unemployed, and the average per capita income was $1,152—less than half the Montana average. He was overruled by the BIA Billings Area Office, which said that bureau regulations required competitive bidding.

For the first two months of 1966, area and agency BIA officials pieced together a public coal permit sale. They persuaded the Northern Cheyenne Tribal Council that the sale was in the tribe's best interests.[19] In three permit sales (1966, 1969, and 1971), the BIA departed from normal Department of the Interior regulations and allowed bidders to claim embarrassingly large parcels of land. The BIA permits included no environmental safeguards.[20]

By the end of the third coal lease sale, over 56% of the reservation had been leased to energy companies and speculators. BIA Area Director James Cannon initiated the coal sales partly in response to the extreme poverty of the Northern Cheyenne Reservation.[21] When Peabody Coal Company bid 12 cents an acre for exploration rights, the BIA considered it a "very good" offer. Naively, BIA considered Cheyenne coal a "white elephant" and wanted to make it as attractive as possible to industry Only later did BIA realize that similar coal already had received bids of $16 to $100 an acre—100 to 1000 times higher than Peabody's bid [22]

Gradually tribal members became more aware of these coal contracts and their ramifications Activists arranged for a busload of tribal members to travel to the Southwest to see for themselves what strip mines looked like and to talk with the Navajo people impacted by them Cheyenne allottees (people who owned reservation land individually) became upset about exploratory drilling on their lands and on Indian burial grounds They formed a landowners association Tribal President Allen Rowland and several council members began asking questions about why their coal was worth only 17 5 cents a ton in royalties when their gravel was selling for 18 cents

In 1972 Consolidation Coal (Consol) returned to the reservation with an astounding offer Consol wanted to build four plants to gasify Cheyenne coal on the tiny reservation, in effect turning it into an industrialized city In exchange, Consol offered millions of dollars in bonuses plus—important for the rural, isolated reservation—a $1 5 million community health center Consol's offer tipped off tribal officials about the true value of their coal [23]

Most Cheyennes agreed that energy development would mean more jobs and a better economy for the reservation When asked what positive changes would result from coal mining, however, nearly one third (104 out of 346 respondents) 'spontaneously said there would be *no* good changes from coal development " The respondents cited many negative effects—most of the same issues with which non-Indians were also concerned—crime, "people pollution," loss of friendships and social ties [25]

The prospect of a reservation overrun by white energy and construction workers was particularly disturbing With only 600 families on the reservation, it was obvious that outsiders would fill most of the new jobs "With more whites coming in, the Cheyenne way of life will soon be forgotten," a young woman said to an interviewer "There will be nothing but half breeds and Indians thinking white, walking around "[26]

The tribal members benefited from the perspective of a newcomer to the reservation, Nancy Owens, who had just finished a dissertation on the energy and construction boom in reservation border towns in the Four Corners region of the Southwest [27] She said, 'The social problems ordinary boomtowns experience are bad enough, but Cheyennes carry over a hundred years of negative experience with the very people who might come to the reservation for jobs The continuing discrimination in nearby white-dominated border towns reaffirms their belief that only where they are in the majority can their lives be led in relative dignity "[28]

Ted Risingsun, cultural leader and occasional member of the tribal council, became a popular spokesman for tribal members In response to the Consol offer, he said, "One thing I might do if the reservation were leased to coal companies is to buy myself the most expensive elkskin scalp shirt anybody ever had You know how our ancestors used to tie scalps on their scalp shirts Well, I would tie pieces of coal on mine I'd buy the biggest pink Cadillac I could find Then I'd drive around the country and dance in all the Indian powwows "

Turning serious, he said, "I think I would rather be poor in my own country, with my own people, with our own way of life than be rich in a torn-up land where I am outnumbered 10 to 1 by strangers "[29]

After months of listening to their constituents and doing their own investigations, the Northern Cheyenne Tribal Council voted 11 to 0 on March 5, 1973, to seek cancellation of all the permits and leases The new tribal attorneys, Alvin J Ziontz and Steven H Chestnut, petitioned the Secretary of Interior saying the permits and leases violated 36 federal regulations [30] According to the tribe's attorney Steven H Chestnut, it was "apparent that the Bureau of Indian Affairs—on whose advice and counsel the tribe relied—had been inept uninformed, and sadly overmatched "[31]

The BIA is part of the Department of Interior, which had improved its regulations governing environmental issues on Indian lands prior to the second and third Northern Cheyenne coal sales The new regulations required study of the land in question "However," Chestnut charged, "the BIA proved itself either unable or unwilling to implement the admirable intent of this regulation "[32] The late 1960s and early 1970s were a period of dramatic changes in the nation's environmental laws, and the Bureau of Indian Affairs far-flung offices apparently couldn't keep up [33]

Secretary of the Interior Rogers C B Morton, reluctant to undermine his own field staff, refused to cancel the leases outright Instead, a year after the petition, on June 4 1974, Morton placed the leases on indefinite hold, a *de facto* victory for the tribe and a face-saving measure for bureau employees

The tribe had taken on some of the most powerful multinational energy companies in the world and won The Cheyennes knew they had defeated BIA bureaucrats in Billings as well "We were *bad* Indians," recalled tribal elder Ted Risingsun, "and they've been punishing us for it ever since "[34] Tribes across the Northern Plains learned from the Cheyennes example Both the neighboring Crow Tribe and the Three Affiliated Tribes of the Fort Berthold Reservation in North Dakota also challenged coal leases and permits on their reservations Other tribes imposed temporary moratoriums on energy development while they studied their situation [35] In 1980, an act of Congress finally cancelled the Cheyenne leases and gave the Northern Cheyennes clear title to their land [36]

In the process of fighting the coal leases, the Northern Cheyenne Tribe formed a clear position in regard to strip mining It also developed a variety of programs and institutions designed to make them less dependent on the federal trustee for guidance The Northern Cheyenne Research Project (NCRP) was founded in 1973 with a grant from the federal Office of Native American Programs The NCRP quickly acquired a wide array of personnel and consultants, ranging from scientists recruited to live and work on the reservation to tribal members researching community and cultural attitudes [37]

The NCRP continued its work throughout the 1970s and early '80s, including natural resource inventories of the reservation and anthropologists' papers that tried to translate the Cheyenne worldview In addition to providing the crucial information needed by the tribe to maintain a credible Tribal Natural Resources Office, the NCRP also documented the attitudes, both positive and negative, of reservation residents toward energy development In the subsequent battle over clean air, the NCRP studies fortified the tribe's position

Clean Air v Jobs

The Northern Cheyennes had good reason to fear the effects of a boomtown They had watched as the tiny coal camp at Colstrip on their northern boundary had exploded in the early 1970s when the Montana Power Company began construction of a new energy center Construction workers, miners, and plant technicians poured into Rosebud County

Vilified as little more than an extended trailer court by many people in the state Colstrip's engineers and blue-collar workers went there because they wanted to earn a living to support their families in a decade when interest rates and inflation had seriously eroded employment rates Once there, they found themselves labeled "people pollution," a term promoted by a sociologist researching the social impacts of development on the region [38]

When the Montana Power Company later proposed construction of two additional generators on its coal-fired power plant, it drove the already volatile Colstrip issue into a full-fledged war in which the Northern Cheyenne Tribe flexed its growing political muscle In 1976, the Northern Cheyenne Tribe objected to Montana Power Company's plans to expand the Colstrip power plant by 1,400 megawatts and by the prospect of several other coal-fired power plants in the area Tribal members discovered that they had a new weapon The Environmental Protection Agency (EPA) had adopted regulations under the Clean Air Act that allowed states and local governments to protect their air

Prevention of Significant Deterioration regulations classified most areas of the United States as Class II, where the air was reasonably clean, but some new pollution was allowable EPA designated national parks and wilderness areas as Class I States and local governments had the option of choosing the Class I designation (which would keep their air relatively pristine) or the Class III designation (which would allow the most pollution)

The Northern Cheyenne Tribe convinced the EPA and eventually the courts that tribes had authority under the law to redesignate and protect their air shed The courts said that the tribe, through the Northern Cheyenne Research Project, had adequately studied the social, environmental, and economic impacts [39] On Sept 16, 1976, the EPA announced that the tribe's Class I standard would be applied to the new generators [40]

The decision infuriated Montana Power Company Engineers had designed Units 3 and 4 to work within the Class II designation, not Class I Montana Power President Joseph McElwain filed a lawsuit against the agency "Somebody, sometime, has to tell the federal government that it can't change the name of the game every 30 minutes without being challenged," McElwain told a reporter "It's too costly for the people and businesses of this nation for the EPA to play games with peoples' pocketbooks and lives "[41]

The Cheyenne petition for clean air met with heavy resistance not only from energy companies but also from the chairman of the neighboring Crow Tribe, Patrick Stands Over Bull, a staunch supporter of coal development on his own reservation [42] Coal was a very divisive issue on the Crow Reservation, and some other tribal members supported the Cheyenne clear air effort, including two members of the Crow Coal Authority, Dale Kindness and Ellis "Rabbit" Knowshisgun [43]

For several years, the Crows had negotiated coal leases with a number of mining companies, including Shell, Amax, Gulf, Westmoreland, and Peabody, although only Westmoreland was actually mining coal in 1977 "Tribal leaders," a *Washington Post* reporter observed, 'have hired a dozen 'public relations men' fluent both in Crow dialect and English to circulate among the far-flung tribal members and convince them of the virtues of coal exploitation ' [44] The Crow dispute spilled over the border to the Northern Cheyenne Reservation and to the EPA offices in Washington, DC

In August, the EPA temporarily shut down the construction site in Colstrip The construction contractor Bechtel immediately laid off 107 workers, and union demonstrators angrily took to the streets of Billings in front of the federal building Their signs said, "Starvation Kills Faster than Bad Air" and 'Out of Work and Hungry? Eat an Environmentalist!" Electricians, heavy equipment operators, pipefitters, laborers, and their families broadcast their message This was not simply a battle between the faceless capitalist exploiters of nature versus the protectors of the earth This was also a fight over who would be allowed to make a living for their families [45]

The Environmental Protection Agency held a series of public meetings in southeastern Montana As expected, the Colstrip meeting consisted mostly of a pep rally for construction A local advocacy group called Montana People for Progress accused the agency of acquiescing to "extremists."[46]

The agency heard different opinions at its hearing in Lame Deer Three of the speakers—Ted Risingsun, Joe Bear, and Sylvester Knowshisgun—were all tribal councilmen All three were about the same age and had grown up as friends Each had become prominent in different churches on the reservation, Risingsun a deacon in the White River Cheyenne Mennonite Church, Knowshisgun a Pentecostal pastor, and Bear a Mormon bishop

But their divergent spiritual paths were not so much differences as preferences, and they knew the Cheyenne heart as well as any Risingsun told the agency of his pride in the label "obstructionist"—the Cheyennes of a century before were called the same thing Bear pointed out that the air was all that was left to the tribe, "we want to keep it " Knowshisgun argued that the government seemed more interested in protecting trophy fishing than in protecting human rights Other speakers, including Cheyenne Native rights activist Gail Small and medicine man Charles Whitedirt, said that the construction in Colstrip would do violence to the tribe, from destroying medicinal plants to undermining tribal sovereignty[47]

The tribe held up construction on the $1 billion Colstrip project for three years, forcing the utilities to install better pollution-control devices Then on Sept 17, 1979, the Montana Supreme Court ruled that construction on Units 3 and 4 could continue While some viewed the construction of the power plants as a defeat for the tribe, the Class I battle had significant benefits locally and nationally As a result of the Northern Cheyennes' Class I air, the company was required to use the best pollution-control technology available at the time Montana Power had to pay for air monitoring stations so the tribe could keep track of whether the plant met its commitments Cheyenne people were trained to monitor the air The company had to meet a quota for the number of Northern Cheyenne employees and had to give preference for Cheyenne contractors[48] Edwin Dahl, the Northern Cheyenne tribal administrator for the agreement and a primary force behind the redesignation decision, said it had resulted in jobs for 200 of the 3,000 resident tribal members and had increased the standard of living on the reservation tenfold[49]

Nationally, the Northern Cheyenne Tribe's action changed forever the way that tribes looked at federal environmental laws The tribe was the first government—state, local, or tribal—in the country to choose Class I Congress adopted regulations in 1977 that formalized the tribal authority for redesignation, thus adding weight to the earlier EPA administrative decision

Once the Cheyenne breached the dam, there was a flood of tribal initiatives to protect reservation air sheds Two other reservations in Montana—Fort Peck and Flathead—obtained Class I redesignations Those tribes also decided to pro-

tect their air quality despite the constraints that it imposed upon their own plans
Fort Peck's Assiniboine and Sioux Tribes were most concerned about coal-fired
power plants, and the Salish and Kootenai Tribe of the Flathead Reservation were
worried about sawmills [50] Later, the Northern Cheyenne Tribe developed its own
Tribal Water Standards under a different law, the Clean Water Act In 2007, the
tribe was one of only a handful of tribes in the country that had established its
own water quality standards [51]

SURFACE V MINERAL OWNERSHIP

Given the mineral wealth that lay just below the surface of Cheyenne country,
the challenges continued One of the factors that makes the energy wars of the
American West so bitter is the "split estate " In much of the West, one landowner
owns the rights to the land's surface and another, the minerals that lay underneath
When the minerals are strip mined, the landowner completely loses the use of
the surface, and other mineral development methods have serious impacts on the
surface, too

Congress had long recognized the potential value of the Northern Cheyenne
coal [52] In 1926, Congress formally allotted the Northern Cheyenne Reservation
This was part of a national policy that opposed communal land ownership and
divided reservation lands up amongst individual tribal members, often opening
the "surplus" reservation land to homesteading

The Cheyenne allotment law specified that the subsurface minerals belonged
to the tribe, but they would belong to the allottees in 50 years Congress apparently believed that by then, the Cheyennes would have been completely integrated
into mainstream American society, and their commitment to tribal or communal
ownership of resources would have disappeared Congress's belief turned out to
be a complete misreading of Native cultures generally and Cheyenne culture in
particular, where land is more than real estate and symbolizes who a person is, not
simply where a person lives [53]

When the mineral ownership was about to shift from tribe to individuals in
1976, the tribe brought the matter to the U S Supreme Court in what became
known as the Hollowbreast Case The nation's highest court confirmed that a
Native community has a vested right to its own natural resources, and the disposi-
tion of those resources would be the decision not of individual landowners but the
tribal government [54] The Hollowbreast decision meant that Native communities
nationwide could be secure in their ownership of their own natural resources

However, the Hollowbreast decision also opened the door to more conflict
between the tribal government and individual landowners In 1980, the Northern
Cheyenne Tribal Council approved a contract with the energy giant Atlantic Rich-

field Company (ARCO) to explore the reservation for oil and gas The conflict created a constitutional crisis on the reservation as the tribe used its governmental powers to protect its proprietary interests in the oil The contract covered the entire reservation, not just specifically tribal lands Landowners, alarmed that their property could be overrun by corporate prospectors, sued in the tribal court to stop the exploration, and when the tribal judge decided the case in favor of the landowners, she was fired by tribal chairman Allen Rowland [55]

Rowland, a fierce opponent of coal development, understood that oil and gas development generally was much less destructive than coal strip mining He was also motivated by the same argument that had moved BIA officials in the 1970s— the extraordinary poverty on the reservation demanded some sort of response, and the only resources available to the Northern Cheyennes were their minerals

The ARCO agreement also won support by a wide margin at the polling place when members voted at two local referenda on the matter Opponents said off-reservation voters—who would receive benefits without suffering the impacts—had swung the vote, heavily influenced by the council's promise to distribute ARCO's $6 million bonus to the members The bitterness of the ARCO deal struck deep A constitutional revision was passed many years later to provide for a separation of powers between the tribal courts and the council, although whether the court is truly independent of the council continued to be an open question [56] The feelings of the traditional community were made clear by the holding of the Sacred Arrow Worship ceremony to pray for assistance and direction in the face of one of the country's most powerful corporations [57]

In the end, ARCO drilled seven holes, all of them dry, and found no oil or gas It left the reservation in 1984 The controversy created a deep rift between some landowners and their elected leaders Yet, as in the Hollowbreast case, the control of reservation resources remained a question for the tribal government, not individual members, to decide [58]

CONCLUSION

American Indian activism since the 1960s is often defined in terms of well-publicized national milestones, such as the takeover of Alcatraz Island in 1969, the Trail of Broken Treaties and the American Indian Movement (AIM)'s occupation of the Bureau of Indian Affairs offices in Washington, DC, in 1972, and the 1973 standoff at Wounded Knee, SD While these events received much attention, the Northern Cheyennes were working behind the scenes toward nationhood, achieving milestones, not headlines

They utilized modern tools to exercise their sovereignty over their land, their air, and their minerals Fighting against some of the most powerful companies in the world, they saved their reservation from being strip mined and turned into an industrial center When sociologist Joane Nagel visited the reservation in 1993 for research on a book on Indian activism, she heard tribal elder Ted Risingsun take a rather unenthusiastic view of AIM and other activist groups [59] For his people had mobilized themselves on their own terms and with their own resources to create their own road to sovereignty

1 Ted Risingsun often quoted Chief Dull Knife's words and provided them in Cheyenne (personal communication)

2 Evans W B, & Peterson R J (1970, July) Decision at Colstrip The Northern Pacific's open-pit mining operation *Pacific Northwest Quarterly* 61(3) 130-141

3 M Holswarth Colstrip resident (personal communication)

4 Foley Brothers Inc *Foley Brothers Inc, an eighty year story* 8

5 Toole, K R (1972) *Twentieth-century Montana A state of extremes* (101) Norman University of Oklahoma Press Howard J K (1943) *Montana high, wide and handsome* (84) New Haven Yale University Press

6 Johnson, C (1988) Electric power copper, and John D Ryan *Montana The Magazine of Western History* 38(4), 28

7 Wolcott, V A (12 November 1925) Colstrips electrical equipment is unusual *Coal Age* 28(20) 663

8 B Tall Bull Northern Cheyenne elder (personal communication)

9 Mike Mansfield Papers University of Montana MS 65, Series III Box 24, folder 16 Beeler and Naddy

10 Ambler, M (1990) *Breaking the iron bonds Indian control of energy development* (p 20) Lawrence University Press of Kansas

11 Hunter, J to Sandoz M 9 September 1953, Mari Sandoz Correspondence (microfilm reel MS00020), Lincoln University of Nebraska

12 Drinnon, R (1987) *Keeper of the concentration camps Dillon S Myer and American racism* (p 237) Berkeley University of California Press

13 W McRae (personal communication)

14 A Spang (personal communication)

15 A Spang (personal communication)

16 Toole K R (1976) *The rape of the Great Plains Northwest America cattle and coal* (pp 50 68) Boston Little Brown and Company

17 Toole, *The rape of the Great Plains* 66-67

18 Ziontz, Pirtle, Morisset & Ernstoff, Attorneys for the Northern Cheyenne Tribe, *Petition of the Northern Cheyenne Tribe to Roger C B Morton Secretary of the Interior, concerning coal leases and permits on their reservation* Seattle Ziontz, Pirtle Morisset & Ernstoff, 1974, II-4

19 Ziontz et al *Petition of the Northern Cheyenne Tribe* II-4

20 Chestnut S H (1979) Coal development on the Northern Cheyenne Reservation In U S Commission on Civil Rights *Energy Resource Development* (p 173) Washington, DC Government Printing Office

21 Toole, *The rape of the Great Plains,* 51-52

22 Ambler, *Breaking the iron bonds,* 62 90

23 Ambler *Breaking the iron bonds,* 65

24 Nordstrom J, Boggs, J P, Owens N J & Sookris, J (1977) *The Northern Cheyenne Tribe and energy development Vol 1 Social Cultural, and Economic Investigations* Lame Deer MT Northern Cheyenne Tribe, 158-159 Tables IV-5 and IV 6

25 *The Northern Cheyenne Tribe and energy development 1* 164-165

26 *The Northern Cheyenne Tribe and energy development 1* 164

27 Owens N (1979) The effects of reservation bordertowns and energy exploitation on American Indian economic development *Research in Economic Anthropology* 2 303-337

28 *The Northern Cheyenne Tribe and energy development,* 1 167

29 Ashabranner B (1982) *Morning star black sun The Northern Cheyenne Indians and America's energy crisis* (pp 92-93) New York Dodd Mead, and Company T Risingsun (personal communication)

30 Toole, *The rape of the Great Plains,* 56-66

31 Chestnut, Coal development on the Northern Cheyenne Reservation, 165-166

32 Chestnut, Coal development on the Northern Cheyenne Reservation 165

We Will Keep our Cheyenne Home Forever

I N LAME DEER, Busby, Birney, Ashland, and Muddy Creek, MT, the Northern
Cheyenne people remember the heroism of their ancestors For them, history
is not just a subject that people study in school and then forget They know
that their people nearly became extinct in the 1880s Nearly every gathering—from
powwows to school board meetings – opens with a prayer and a reference to the
long journey from Indian Territory back to Montana The official tribal stationery
with pictures of Chiefs Dull Knife and Little Wolf on the top, says, "Out of defeat
and exile they led us back to Montana and won our Cheyenne home, which we
will keep forever "

However, there is less awareness on the reservation and elsewhere of the national precedents that the Northern Cheyenne Tribe and its people have set in the
20th century They have broken new ground for tribal sovereignty in education
and environmental law, and they have been pioneers in social justice for both Indian and non-Indian communities Some of these milestones are described earlier
in this book, and this chapter provides more recent examples

•In July 1972, the Northern Cheyenne Tribe became one of the first tribes
in the country to transform a Bureau of Indian Affairs school into a tribally-con-
trolled school during the new Indian-controlled school movement

•The Northern Cheyenne Tribal Council in 1974 started a revolution in
American Indian energy policy, preventing some of the largest multinational energy companies in the world from strip mining the reservation and turning it
into an industrial complex Other tribes subsequently followed the Cheyennes'
example and challenged their coal leases on the same basis

•In 1976, the tribe brought one of the state's most powerful corporations to
its knees for several years by utilizing federal environmental law to protect the
reservation airshed The Environmental Protection Agency stopped construction
of the Colstrip coal-fired power plant expansion and forced the utilities to install

costly air pollution control technology The tribe was the first in the nation to utilize this provision of national environmental laws, and today more than a dozen other tribes manage their own air quality programs

• In 1986, Northern Cheyenne elder William Tall Bull was one of the Indian leaders who demanded protection for American Indian graves and the return of "spiritual beings' housed in museum storerooms He helped U S Sen John Melcher write the Native American Graves Protection and Repatriation Act in 1990 and later was appointed by the Secretary of Interior to serve as the only American Indian on the committee that wrote the regulations for the law His passing was noted in the Congressional record by U S Sen Ben Nighthorse Campbell March 19, 1996

• In 1991, the Federal Reserve Board sent a shock wave through the banking world when it ruled in favor of Native Actions challenge of the First Interstate Bank merger It forced bankers nationwide to look at how they could better serve communities

The Land in the 21st Century

As they enter the 21st century, the Northern Cheyenne people draw upon these victories and the strength of their ancestors to face continuing threats to their land, culture, and people They must battle constant pressure from energy development companies, internal strife about development, and outsiders ignorance about what it means to be an American Indian in the United States today The Northern Cheyenne Tribe became everyone's favorite Indians for a period of time in the 1970s when they turned down millions of dollars for their coal The words of Ted Risingsun (a respected elder, Korean War hero, and a direct descendant of Chief Dull Knife) were cited widely by environmentalists "I think I would rather be poor in my own country, with my own people, with our own way of life than be rich in a torn-up land where I am outnumbered ten to one by strangers "[1] The Cheyenne's courageous battle to protect their land mystified many at the time and led to a romanticized image of the Cheyenne that haunted them later

With all the money offered to the Cheyenne for their coal in the 1970s, why didn't they just take the money and move? Outsiders often misunderstand the importance of reservations to American Indian people, seeing it as a form of apartheid where Indian people are segregated from others As a result of this misunderstanding misguided "friends" of the Indians have tried for more than 500 years to integrate them into the American system of individual land ownership Often these attempts have been combined with efforts to take their lands and resources While many have been motivated by greed, others have sincerely misunderstood the Indians' attachment to their land People who considered themselves friends of the Indians have championed the cause of assimilation with missionary-like zeal, saying "We ought to give them freedom we ought to give them liberty, and we ought to give them their rights "

So why do the Northern Cheyennes choose to live on their reservation Not all do—about one-third of all American Indians live on reservations and one-half of all enrolled Northern Cheyennes live on their reservation [2] More might return if there were more jobs Those who stay or return have various reasons They love their land They stay to be with their families and so their children can benefit from time spent with family elders They participate in tribal traditional and religious activities They get more medical and economic benefits from the federal and tribal governments than members who live elsewhere Many feel strongly that they want to serve their people and often leave to complete their education, later returning to work It is the only place where they can expect to hear and speak their language and be surrounded by people of their culture Many of their ancestors are buried there

Culture may not materialize in the form that outsiders expect Tribal members may wear silk suits with their beads and braids and have degrees from Harvard or Boston University Their culture often thrives within them, invisible to outsiders, not necessarily hanging across their chests in a medicine bag All cultures face pressure toward mainstream values from television, Nintendo, glossy fashion magazines, etc But the land gives American Indian people a better chance of retaining important aspects of their culture and language

Within their boundaries, the Northern Cheyenne have been able to retain nearly complete ownership, unlike most other tribes in the West Elsewhere, non-Indians acquired large percentages of the land ownership as a result of homestead laws and allotment laws passed by Congress in the late 1800s and early 1900s For example, the Salish and Kootenai Tribes of the Flathead Reservation in Montana lost over half of their reservation, mostly the rich agricultural land of the Flathead Valley [3] Fortunately for the Cheyenne, their land was not as desirable for agriculture Then in the 1950s, under the far-sighted leadership of John Woodenlegs, the Northern Cheyenne Tribe developed an unallotment program to prevent allotments (owned by individual Indians) from being sold outside the tribe The tribe was assisted by the Association on American Indian Affairs (a nonprofit organization formed in the 1920s dedicated to working with Indians) [4] As a result of the Hollowbreast U S Supreme Court decision discussed in the energy chapter in this book, the tribe also controls the minerals under the reservation

However, tribal members must continue to worry about threats to its land cultural resources, and air from development on the boundary and outside, especially in the area of the Tongue River Valley In 2004, Fidelity Exploration & Production Company filed a lawsuit in federal court to determine if the Northern

Cheyenne Tribe owned half of the Tongue River Bed The energy firm had obtained several oil and gas leases along the Tongue River from the state of Montana in 2002 Fidelity wanted to prove that if the state owned the land, then Fidelity's leases applied to that land beneath the river

Tongue River has historical and spiritual significance to the tribe The area was their last sanctuary for retaining their unique cultural identity A cottonwood grove along the Tongue River floodplain was used as a camp from at least the 1800s until 1930 Religious ceremonies, including the annual renewal of the Medicine Bundles, took place at this camp The Northern Cheyenne recognize the spiritual nature of water in general and of the Tongue River in particular They make cloth and tobacco offerings to the river Important ceremonial events, such as fasts, sweats, and the Sun Dance, Sacred Hat, and Ghost Dance ceremonies have been performed in the Tongue River valley Spirits live in the springs there [5] William Tall Bull in 1991 testified that as development occurs in the Powder River region, the Northern Cheyenne people will have fewer and fewer undisturbed places to go to collect ceremonially significant pigments and plants He told them that off reservation pollution from the Colstrip power plants was making some medicinal plants unsafe [6]

In November 2007, the 9th Circuit Court of Appeals ended the Fidelity riverbed dispute by dismissing the company's case because the statute of limitations had expired [7] Once again, the tribe was successful in retaining its land rights However, Fidelity's development plans continued on the other side of the river That area continued to be threatened in 2007 by coal bed methane development and by the Montco coal-strip mine and railroad [8]

South of the reservation, coal bed methane development had begun Skyrocketing fossil fuel prices and new technologies made methane the boom fuel of the new century in Montana, Wyoming, and Colorado It was replacing coal for electric power generation To produce methane involves drilling a grid of wells that pump the water out of the coal beds and discharge the methane It drains irreplaceable aquifers in an already arid land and discharges water full of salts, minerals, ammonia, and other substances Very little is known about how draining so many aquifers will affect the groundwater system, according to Native Action, a grassroots organization based in Lame Deer involved in protecting Northern Cheyenne resources for over 20 years [9]

The tribe, Native Action, and the Northern Plains Resource Council sued the federal government over coalbed methane development in the Tongue River Valley and the Power River Basin areas outside the reservation, and as of 2007, they had prevented it Gail Small of Native Action said, "Over the years, the tribe has used its limited dollars to protect the region from massive exploitation This has given us time to get our young people educated The elders are ready to pass on the land to the next generation and hope they are ready to manage it."[10]

So far, the tribal government has turned its back on coal mining on the reservation, and the oil and gas exploration has been unsuccessful. However, there is no guarantee that the tribe can resist forever. In a referendum election in November 2006, a majority of people actually voted for coal development (664 to 572). The topic of coalbed methane was more hotly discussed at the time, and more than twice as many people voted against developing coalbed methane on the reservation (841 to 365).[11]

THE ECONOMY AND HEALTH

SOME SAY THAT THE NORTHERN CHEYENNE PEOPLE CONTINUE TO PAY A HORRIBLE PRICE FOR THEIR LAND AND THAT CUSTER DID LESS VIOLENCE TO THE CHEYENNE PEOPLE THAN A HUNDRED YEARS OF POVERTY. HUNGER IS A DAILY REALITY THERE. A SURVEY IN 2001 found that over two-thirds of the households experienced occasional hunger, and one-third experienced persistent hunger.[12] Nearly 50% of Cheyenne families live under the poverty level. With few businesses on the reservation, unemployment is always high; it fluctuates between 60% and 85% because of the number of seasonal jobs.[13]

Even amongst Indian people, twice as many Northern Cheyennes are poor, and they are four times as likely to be poor compared with all people in the country (26% of all American Indians and Alaska Natives live below the poverty line compared with 12% of all the people in the country).[14] The reasons for the poverty vary. Millions of dollars flow into the reservations each year in the form of contracts, grants, loans, and salaries. If the local economy has not been developed, most of this money flows out again, spent at non-Indian owned businesses such as grocery stores and car dealers, paid in federal taxes, and invested in banks far from the community.

Poverty correlates with poor health nationwide. A report on federal funding in Indian Country published by the U.S. Civil Rights Commission in 2003 said that American Indian people are 650% more likely to die from tuberculosis than other Americans, 318% more likely to die from diabetes, 670% more likely to die from alcoholism, and 204% more likely to suffer accidental death when compared with other groups. It blamed such health disparities on poverty, poor education, and lack of access to health care. The Indian Health Service spent 50% less per person ($1,600 per year) for comprehensive health services in its hospitals and health clinics compared with public and private health insurance plans, according to the report. In fact, the federal government spent more on health care for prisoners than for American Indians.[15]

Lesser people might be daunted by these problems, but the Northern Cheyennes have never complacently accepted their fate When left without any health care facility, they demanded and received a new clinic When denied the banking services most communities take for granted, they demanded and received their own bank When they were the only area of their size to lack a high school in the whole state, they fought for and won their own high school The high school is now part of an educational system that is attempting to change the future of the reservation, one graduate at a time

Northern Cheyenne Health Clinic

Health care is one of the most essential services in rural America When the U S Government signed a treaty with the Northern Cheyenne and Arapahoe Tribes in 1868 it agreed to provide health care, [16] but health services in the community have never been adequate for the needs Health care was a function of the Department of Interior until 1955 when the Indian Health program was transferred to the Public Health Service [17]

In Lame Deer, a hospital had been built in 1926 at a time when various diseases had reached epidemic proportions on the reservation, as described in the education history chapter In 1955, the hospital was reduced to a clinic The poor services provided by the hospital and its downgraded status as a clinic forced the Cheyennes, who continued to be ravaged by tuberculosis even in the 1950s, to travel all the way to Crow Agency to seek treatment Author Mari Sandoz, who was in the area researching her novel about the Cheyennes' flight from exile, *Cheyenne Autumn*, felt compelled to write President Harry S Truman about the conditions [18]

In 1975, the Indian Health Service and the Northern Cheyenne Tribe sought and received funds to build a new clinic Twenty years later, however, this clinic burned to the ground in May 1996 The destruction of the clinic created a health crisis for the Northern Cheyenne people Initially, services were scattered through out the community and were housed in temporary trailers and buildings Some services were transferred to the Crow/Northern Cheyenne Hospital in Crow Agency, 45 miles away

Out of the ashes of the old clinic, hope sprang for a new, larger facility Because of the fire, the Northern Cheyenne Service was given higher priority to receive a new facility Planning began immediately The Northern Cheyenne Board of Health contracted to build a new, $14 4 million clinic under federal self-determination statutes Three years after the old clinic burned the new, 62,000 square-feet Northern Cheyenne Health Clinic was completed in 1999 The number of staff was doubled, and new services were added

Donita Sioux, the project coordinator for the Northern Cheyenne Health

Clinic, told *Indian Country Today*, "The health services are now under one roof, and patients are treated in a sparkling building that rivals medical clinics in the state's largest cities The facility also includes a rock-floored healing room that's designed like a sweat lodge It's a place where families and patients can go to pray or otherwise find solace The design is more culturally relevant to the tribe, to the people "[19] In 2007, the clinic continued to serve the needs of the Northern Cheyenne people

First Interstate Bank

In the late 1980s, Native Action recognized the need for the tribe to be able to control its own money and leverage it to build an economy They hired a banker and local researchers to conduct an economic survey, which discovered that 90 people on the reservation were either in business or wanted to open their own businesses—if they could obtain financing Some of the entrepreneurs were hair stylists, fur buyers, and tax accountants, they wanted to start video stores, expand their ranches, and start construction companies "There was a fascinating array of talent that we never realized we had," Native Action Executive Director Gail Small said [20] The survey looked at all the money coming into the reservation and explored what could be done with that money if it were not spent or invested outside the boundaries

First Interstate Bank, a family-owned corporation based in Billings, MT, claimed to serve the reservation However, the reservation lacked even an Automatic Teller Machine (ATM) Few people could get loans, partially because lenders believed they could not collect collateral in case of default on the reservation Native Action researched a little known provision of federal banking law, the 1977 Community Reinvestment Act (CRA), which requires banks to meet the credit needs of low- and moderate-income people in local communities Up until that time, it was just a piece of paper that had never been used After First Interstate Bank applied to federal regulators to merge with a sister bank in Wyoming, however, Native Action charged the bank with redlining the reservation In January 1990, the organization formally accused the bank's branch in Colstrip, MT, of profiting from Northern Cheyenne transactions without providing enough loans to tribal members First Interstate officials were infuriated at the uppity organization The Federal Reserve Board sent a mediator to Montana to see if agreement could be reached It could not

So on Oct 7, 1991, the Board of Governors of the Federal Reserve for the first time in history rejected a merger application solely on the bank's failure to satisfy requirements of the CRA It said the Colstrip bank was not adequately serving the credit needs of the Northern Cheyenne Reservation The vote was three to

The tribe's elders often ask to deal directly with Barbara Braided Hair, branch manager of First Interstate Bank in Lame Deer, who has helped them feel more comfortable about using a bank for the first time. (Photo by Kathleen Beartusk)

two with Alan Greenspan casting the tie breaking vote. The decision rocked the banking world. A front-page story in *American Banker*, the New York City-based magazine, said the decision was a warning to all holding companies nationwide to monitor the community-lending records of its subsidiaries.[23] The front page of the *Billings Gazette* proclaimed, "Fed Sides with Native Action." First Interstate, the third largest commercial bank in Montana with $629 million in assets, had to meet the demands of the Northern Cheyennes. It was the first time that teeth had been put into the CRA.

By then, the tribal members had organized a Chamber of Commerce to take the lead in the negotiations with the bank. The tribal members wanted an ATM and eventually their own bank. They wanted $10 million in new loans, and they wanted a bank training program so that local people could fill the jobs at the bank. After holding up the merger for nearly two years, the agreement was signed Sept. 18, 1992, by representatives of the diverse groups that eventually got involved in the process—the bank, Native Action, the Northern Cheyenne Area Chamber of

Commerce, the Northern Cheyenne Tribal Council, and the Northern Cheyenne Livestock Association [22]

To make the bank possible, the Northern Cheyenne Tribe had to enact some important governmental changes By referendum, the tribal membership passed a reorganization that separated legislative, judicial, and executive branches [23] To make lending more attractive on the reservation, the tribe adopted a commercial code Each state has a Uniform Commercial Code to guarantee legal obligations and protect property interests in a uniform manner As separate jurisdictions, Indian reservations must provide a similar guarantee in order to attract business investments Native Action drafted a Tribal Uniform Commercial Code, which after much public review and comment, was adopted by the Northern Cheyenne Tribal Council in 1998 The code provides consistency and fairness to debtor/creditor relationships on the reservation, while recognizing the tribal courts and the tribe's unique cultural heritage [24]

While they started out as adversaries, First Interstate Bank and the tribe became allies Within three and a half years, First Interstate Bank reached the agreed open lending goal of $10 million The ATM machine had so much use that it made First Interstate realize a bank would work there First Interstate Bank developed a manager trainee program that's targeting Native Americans and was working on an internship program to draw recruits from tribal colleges A tribal member, Barbara Braided Hair, became the branch manager, and she helped build trust amongst tribal members The bank also helped tribal members both on and off reservations obtain housing loans [25] "If (the Lame Deer) community is not successful, the branch won't be successful," Maria Valandra told *Indian Country Today* Valandra is an enrolled member of the Chippewa-Cree Tribe who also served as the company's vice president for community development "I believe the CRA is not something we just comply with It's another way that we can give back to our communities "

The bank became involved in several programs on the Northern Cheyenne Reservation to provide financial education, including going to housing fairs to promote home ownership programs and teaching kids how to save The branch hosted a "minibank" in Lame Deer schools, which was operated by students who set their own policies and handled cash The money went into individual accounts at First Interstate Bank that could only be accessed by students [26] Thus the bank invested in tomorrow's entrepreneurs, business owners, and family financial managers who may continue to transform the local economy Asked about what led to Native Action's success with this project Small said, "You have to include everybody to achieve anything " The process involved local business people, both Indian and non-Indian, Montana Legal Services, the school superintendent, and the tribal chairman at the time, Edwin Dahl

Conclusion

The Northern Cheyenne people do not spend much time congratulating themselves on the milestones they have achieved in the national arena. They face too many problems in their communities everyday to do that. Nevertheless, knowledge of these victories can fortify them if ever they feel daunted. William Tall Bull used to say, "We are the ancestors of those yet to be born." Now in the 21st century Cheyenne people are still making history, fighting against all odds for their people, and they have many non-Indian friends by their sides. Today's warriors are lawyers, doctors, nurses, teachers, professors, language scholars, religious leaders, activists, students, and janitors. Many are invisible to outsiders, and their dedication and creativity may not be known by their community members. Instead, they are quietly doing their jobs with an eye to not only the past but also the future of their people.

1 Ashabranner, B. (1982) *Morning star, black sun: The Northern Cheyenne Indians and America's energy crisis* (pp. 92-93). New York: Dodd, Mead, and Company and T. Risingsun (personal communication)

2 The total number of enrolled was 8,500 and the total number on the reservation was 4,200. Tobacco/gas tax reimbursement (June 2006) *The Nation: Tribal Report of the Northern Cheyenne Nation* 1(7), 4

3 William, B. (1996) *Montana's Indians Yesterday and Today.* Helena, MT: Farcountry Press. p. 120

4 Weist, T. (1977) *A History of the Cheyenne People* (pp. 196-197). Billings: Montana Council for Indian Education

5 *Final Statewide Oil and Gas Environmental Impact Statement*

6 In March 2007 the Colstrip coal-fired power plant owners were forced to install equipment to cut greenhouse gases based upon the demands of the tribe (Johnson, C. (2007, March 24) EPA, tribe, plants settle dispute. *The Billings Gazette*.) The Tall Bull arguments are contained in the *Final Statewide Oil and Gas Environmental Impact Statement and Proposed Amendment of the Powder River and Billings Resource Management Plans.* Washington, DC: Department of Interior, January 2003. Retrieved Dec. 11, 2007 from http://www.mt.blm.gov/mcfo/cbm/eis/NCheyenneNarrativeReport/Chap7.pdf

7 Tongue River ruling upheld (2007, Nov. 8) *The Billings Gazette.* Retrieved Nov. 8, 2007 from http://www.billingsgazette.net/articles/2007/11/08/news/state/25-tongueriver.txt

8 *Native Action 20th Anniversary Report, 1984-2007* (2008) Lame Deer, MT: Native Action

9 *Native Action 20th Anniversary Report*

10 Small, G. (personal communication), Jan. 15, 2008

11 Retrieved Jan. 15, 2008 from http://www.cheyennenation.com/news06.html

12 Davis, J., Hiwalker, R., Ward, C., Feinauer, E., Youngstrom, C. & Lemperle, M. (Oct. 2001) The relationship of food assistance program participation to nutritional and health status, diabetes risk and food security among the Northern Cheyenne (Report to USDA) Ambler, M. (Summer 2002) Rita Hiwalker: Confronting the reality of food and hunger *Tribal College Journal* 13(4), 30-31

13 Bureau of the Census. Census 2000 Summary File 3 (SF 3)

14 Ogunwole, S. U. (2006) *We the People: American Indians and Alaska Natives in the United States.* Washington, DC: U.S. Census Bureau. pp. 11-12

15 U.S. Civil Rights Commission (2003) *A Quiet Crisis: Federal Funding and Unmet Needs in Indian Country.* (No. 005-907-00596-1) Washington, DC: U.S. Civil Rights Commission

16 Kappler, C. (1972) *Indian Treaties 1778-1883.* Washington, DC: Interland Publishing, Inc.

17 Remarks by Commissioner of Indian Affairs Glenn L. Emmons (1957, October 30) Department of the Interior Information Service. p. 1. NARA, RG 75 Records of the Bureau of Indian Affairs, Northern Cheyenne Agency, Lame Deer, MT; Decimal Subject Files, 1926-1952, Box 1 Trans. From 10NS-075-97-013

18 Mari Sandoz to Harry S Truman 10 October 1949, Mari Sandoz Correspondence (microfilm reel MS00016, University of Nebraska, Lincoln)

19 Northern Cheyenne Health Clinic Completed (1999, Nov 15) *Indian Country Today*, 2

20 G Small (personal communication) Dec 21 2007

21 Braitman, F , (1991, Oct 10) CRA report trips merger in Montana *American Banker* 156(197) 1

22 Community Reinvestment Program Mutual Agreement of Cooperation and Understanding (1992, Sept 18)

23 Shay B (2003 March 16) Banking on tradition Northern Cheyenne Reservation gets own bank *The Billings Gazette* Retrieved Dec 7, 2007 from http //billingsgazette net/articles/2003/03/16/business/export99468 txt

24 *Native Action 20th Anniversary Report*

25 Selden R (2002 Jan 31) Prodded by federal law, bank finds good business on reservation *Indian Country Today* Retrieved Dec 7 2007, from http //www indiancountry com/content cfm?id=1012731775

26 Shay, Banking on tradition

Contributors

MARJANE AMBLER WROTE the Coming Home chapter and the concluding chapter (We Will Keep our Cheyenne Home Forever) She first visited the Northern Cheyenne Reservation in 1974 as a journalist covering the Northern Cheyenne coal lease controversy Since then she has specialized in American Indian natural resource and education issues From 1995 until 2006, she was the editor and publisher of the *Tribal College Journal,* a quarterly magazine covering the 35 tribal colleges in the American Indian Higher Education Consortium In 1990, the University Press of Kansas published her book, *Breaking the Iron Bonds Indian Control of Energy Development*

Kathleen B Beartusk took many of the photographs in this book and helped prepare other graphic images A member of the Northern Cheyenne Tribe, she has worked for Chief Dull Knife College (CDKC) for 26 years She received her associate degree from CDKC in 1993 She does a lot of design and desktop publishing for the college A fifth generation descendant of Chief Dull Knife, she has five children ages 19 through 34 She raised them as a single mom Four of her children got degrees from or are beginning their educational journeys at Chief Dull Knife College Her oldest, Adam, is now working on his Master's in Business Administration Her other son, Uriah Two Two, 28, is doing his third tour in Iraq He went into the Army right out of high school She has six grandchildren

Joan Hantz wrote the chapters on Early Education, The Girl Who Saved her Brother, and Balloon Bomb in Lame Deer, and she contributed research to the Coming Home chapter A Montana native, she is a graduate of the University of Montana She received her Library Science Degree from the University of Arizona She has worked in the library profession for 25 years and has been library director at the Di John Woodenlegs Library in Lame Deer for nearly six years She met her husband while attending the University of Montana They have been married for 25 years and have two sons Hantz first became involved with this project when

Dr Richard E Little Bear asked her to do research at the National Archives and Records Administration in Denver She came across many documents with names and places that she recognized Making contacts and interviewing folks in the area was also satisfying to her She hopes that the children of Montana will gain a sense of the Cheyenne community from this book

Richard E Little Bear wrote the Preface and the Language chapter and edited all of the chapters He was born in Lame Deer and was raised in Busby until he was 15 years of age He was primarily raised by his Grandma Rosa Little Bear He attended Northern Cheyenne Tribal Schools (then known as the Tongue River Boarding School) until the eighth grade He then attended high school in Lind, WA, where he was the only American Indian student for three years He graduated from Lind High, attended Centralia Community College, Wenatchee Valley College in Washington State, and Bethel College in Kansas, from which he earned a Bachelor's Degree in English He earned a Master's in Educational Administration from Montana State University in Bozeman, MT and a Doctorate in Educational Administration from Boston University in Boston, MA Since 1996 he has been employed at Chief Dull Knife College, first as the dean of cultural affairs, then as the acting president, then as the president, and now as the dean of cultural affairs and the president He is married to Jan Little Bear who works for the Northwest Regional Educational Laboratory in Portland, OR Between them, they share five children and five grandchildren

Patti Means wrote the article about Joseph Whitewolf She also contributed research for several chapters, including the concluding chapter (We Will Keep our Cheyenne Home Forever), Chief Dull Knife College chapter, the tribal presidents list in the appendix, and the Early Education chapter A graduate of Chief Dull Knife College, she has worked there for 10 years, first at the library and then as the student support services coordinator An enrolled Northern Cheyenne, she has lived on the reservation most of her life She and her husband, David, have three sons (Jarrad, Chauncey, and Kale) and four grandchildren She said she has enjoyed working on this project, especially doing the research

Mina Seminole wrote the chapters on Northern Cheyenne Sacred Sites and Objects Cheyenne Peace Pipe, and District Names She contributed research on the Coming Home chapter She is an enrolled member of the Northern Cheyenne Tribe She enjoyed working on the project because in her youth, she heard many stories from her parents and grandparents Through her research on this project, she became even more appreciative of the ancestors' sacrifices so that generations of Cheyenne people can continue Although she has left the reservation for short periods for education and employment opportunities, her family ties always brought her back home She comes from a family of 12 children, and she is the second oldest During her high school years, she went to a boarding school in Flandreau, SD

After graduation her desire for education and adventure took her to Cleveland, OH, where she attended business school. She met her husband there, he is from the Omaha Tribe in Nebraska. They have 3 children, 13 grandchildren, and 2 great grandchildren. When she started work at Chief Dull Knife College in 2005, her desire to take college classes became a reality. In May 2008, she planned to receive her Associate of Arts degree in Native American Studies.

Linwood Tall Bull wrote the Native Plants chapter. He is an enrolled member of the Northern Cheyenne Tribe and a descendent of Tall Bull, the leader of the Dog Soldiers who was killed at Summit Springs in 1869. Linwood Tall Bull is a Vietnam Era veteran as well as a Headsman for the Dog Soldiers Society, an ancient society that has always protected and preserved the ways of the people. He follows in the footsteps of his father (William Tall Bull), teaching the healing qualities of plants and teaching Ethnobotany at Chief Dull Knife College. He believes that Indian Education for All is one of the best things happening in Montana schools today. Every tribe in Montana and throughout the United States has a colorful, interesting history, strong stories and legends, knowledge about plants and healing, and survival skills. Knowing more about each other will help non-Indian and Indian children learn to live together well, he believes. When they start to learn more about Indian history and culture, all children in our schools will be getting an education about the best of both worlds. That is why he is proud to work on this Tribal Histories Project.

Carol Ward wrote the Contemporary Education and co-wrote the Chief Dull Knife College chapters. She received her Ph.D. from the University of Chicago in 1992. Her interest in American Indian education led to her work as a research specialist for the Administration for Native Americans in Washington, DC, for five years. In the early 1980s she worked as a consultant to Chief Dull Knife College and then as a staff and faculty member from 1987-1990. As a result of this work, she completed a dropout study on the Northern Cheyenne Indian Reservation, which was published as a monograph, *Native Americans in the School System* by AltaMira Press in 2005. She joined the sociology faculty at Brigham Young University in 1990 and teaches classes in racial and ethnic relations, sociology of education, community, and qualitative and survey methods. She has continued to work with the Northern Cheyenne over the last 17 years on issues related to K-12 and higher education, substance abuse recovery, and the effects of welfare reform on food insecurity and health conditions. These projects have involved community surveys as well as interviews with members of the Northern Cheyenne community. She is currently conducting research concerning the effectiveness of recent innovations in the math and science curriculum and expansion of student services at Chief Dull Knife College.

Bill Wertman co-wrote the Chief Dull Knife College (CDKC) chapter and contributed research to the Coming Home chapter. He is vice president of the college, where he has been employed for 28 years. Prior to his employment at CDKC, he was the director of student development at Busby Schools for seven years. He earned his bachelor's degree from Eastern Montana College and his master's degree from Montana State University-Bozeman. A life-long resident of southeastern Montana, Wertman has two daughters (Jodean and Lindsey) and a son (Devin), all of whom have completed studies at CDKC. Devin is currently pursuing a bachelor's degree at Rocky Mountain College. Wertman enjoys working at the college because he likes assisting students as they explore and ultimately realize their educational dreams. Each day brings new challenges and opportunities for both personal and institutional growth.

Dave Wilson wrote the Agriculture and the Energy chapters and helped research several of the other chapters. He has a Bachelor's of Arts in History, a Master's of Arts in Classics from the University of Kansas, and a Ph D. in History from Brigham Young University. He began working at Chief Dull Knife College in 1985, was on the staff of the tribal college from 1986 to 1990, and since then has considered Rosebud County as his home. He is now an assistant professor of History and American Indian Studies at Utah Valley State College in Orem. He says that his "real" Ph D. came from the Northern Cheyenne Reservation, where his 'committee" consisted of William Tall Bull, Ted Risingsun, Florence Whiteman Lee and Juanita Lonebear, Alonzo Spang, and Richard Tall Bull. The research for these chapters was based mostly on archival sources, with a few interviews.

APPENDIX A

Northern Cheyenne Veterans List

THIS LIST WAS compiled primarily by Janet Mullin The people who worked on this list tried to include everyone, but there are undoubtedly omissions, especially in the list from the 1880s If someone has been omitted, contact Janet Mullin at the Jessie Mullin Picture Museum in Lame Deer (406) 477-6460

Last Name	First Name	Date Enlisted	Date Discharged	Branch	Source
Allen	Dean	1977	1979	Air Force	
American Horse	Allen Ward			Navy Korea	Legion
American Horse	Francis	12/11/1968			
American Horse	Roger	5/22/1962	6/2/1969		
American Horse	Marvin			Army	Museum
American Horse	Terry			Marine	
American Horse	Ward				Newspaper
Archambeau	Irene	1941	2/??/1951	Army	
Atwood	David, Sr	1950		Army	Museum
Atwood	Herbert W				
Atwood	Waldo				Museum
Buhr	Frances			Marine	
Baldeagle	Hugh			Army	
Barrus	Hunter	1998	2003	Navy	Museum
Baylor	Teresa Trusty				
Bear	Joe, Sr	1/11/1950	./14/1954	Army	
Bearchum	Benjamin				Newspaper
Bearchum	Ella Jean				
Bearchum	Frank Jr				Legion
Bearchum	Jerome Jr	11/25/1946	4/16/1947	Army	
Bearchum	Robert Sr			Marine	Museum
Bearchum	Tyrone			Navy	Museum
Bearchum	Wallace, Sr	10/16/1930	4/10/1954	Army	Legion
Bearcomesout	Joe, Sr	1951	1954	Army	Legion
Bearcomesout	Charles			Marine	
Bearcomesout	Lorelie			Army	
Bearcomesout	Michael, Jr			Marine	
Bearcomesout	Peter Harold I	1997	2001	Army	

Last Name	First Name	Date Enlisted	Date Discharged	Branch	Source
Bearquiver	Edmond			Army	Museum
Bearquiver	Frank Jr				
Bearquiver	Frank Sr			Army	Museum
Bearquiver	James				Legion
Beartusk	Jerome, Jr				Legion
Beartusk	Kenneth	2/2/1942	10/20/1945		Newspaper
Beartusk	Ralph				Legion
Beartusk	Jerome, Jr				Newspaper
Beartusk	Reuben	1951		Army	Museum
Beckman	Eugene	4/20/1951	11/13/1953	Air Force	Family
Beaudreau	Albert				
Bement	Albert R			Marine	
Bement	Clarence				Legion
Bement	Clarence, Mickey				Army
Bement	Myron W	2004	2005	Army	
Bement	Raymond				Legion
Big Back	Eugene	1950		Army	Museum
Big Back	Eugene Jr	1977	1981	Army	
Big Back	Charles	1890	1892	Casey Scout	
Big Back	James			Marine	Museum
Big Back	Kimberly	1990		Marine	Museum
Big Back	Robert				Legion
Big Foot Gardner	Joseph	1950		Army	Museum
Big Foot Gardner	Willie				Legion
Big Hawk	Doug				Museum
Big Hawk	William			Army	
Big Head	Clayton Lee				
Big Head	Clifford			Army	Museum
Big Headman	William				Legion
Big Lefthand	Perry			Army	
Big Lefthand	Rafeal			Army	
Big Medicine	Joseph			Army	Museum
Bigback	Kimberly				
Brady	Alex	1965			Museum
Brady	Dana				
Brady	Steve				
Bighead	William Grover				
Bites	James	1/7/1952		Marine	Legion
Bixby	Lawrence				Legion
Bixby	Lloyd		1951	Killed, Korea	Museum
Bixby	James				Legion
Bixby	Sam				Legion
Black Horse	Reuben	11/27/1890	5/26/1891	Scout	
Blackstone	Louis	1950		Army	Legion
Blackstone	Charles	11/27/1890	5/26/1891	Troop C	
Blackstone	Mathew			Marine	Museum
Bobtail Horse				Scout	Museum
Bolson	Frank	9/17/1940	7/15/1945	Army	Legion
Bolson	Roy Guy				Legion
Brady	Alex	1965			Museum
Brady	Arnold			Marine	
Brady	Dana	1997	2001		
Brady	Deanna			Marine	
Brady	Gilbert	11/16/1969	8/22/1972	Marine	
Brady	Joe			Army	
Brady	Joel			Army	

Last Name	First Name	Date Enlisted	Date Discharged	Branch	Source
Brady	Marlin	1985	1986	Army	
Brady	Maynard Sr				
Brady	Merlin			Navy	
Brady	Otto				Legion
Brady	Raymond	3/3/1943	12/27/1945	Army	Legion
Brady	Steven G			Marine	
Brady	Wilson				Legion
Braine	Carl				
Braine	Gary			Army	
Brave Love	Greg				Museum
Brien	Kenneth Buddy	1943	1945	Army	
Brien	Phillip			Navy	Museum
Brien	Ronald Bruce				
Buffalohorn	John	5/3/1870	4/2/1891	Troop A	Legion
Bullcoming	Dana			Marine	
Bullcoming	Donald, Jr			Marine	
Bullcoming	Dwight	1973	1975	Marine	Museum
Bullcoming	George			Army	Museum
Bullcoming	Garriet				
Bullcoming	Tom			Army	Museum
Bullsheep	Martin				
Burgess	Fritz	1966		Army	
Burns	Bernadette			Navy	
Burns	George Dempsey				Museum
Burns	George E	1/11/1951	1/10/1955	Air Force	Legion
Burns	Kyle	7/1/2002		Marine	
Burns	Robert, Sr	1952	1956	Navy	Museum
Cady	George			Army	
Cady	Klee			Army	
Cain	Leslie E			Air Force	
Charette	Earl			Navy	
Chavez	Daniel			Army	Museum
Chavez	John			Army	Museum
Chavez	Thornton			Army	Museum
Chavez	William			Army	Museum
Clubfoot	Huge			Marine	Museum
Clubfoot Adams	Peter	11/16/1945	11/15/1948	Army	Legion
Cooley	Francis				
Corneliusen	Robin	1/1/1974	1/1/1980	Army	Museum
Crazymule	James				Legion
Crazymule	Kenneth	12/5/1968	3/6/1974		
Crazymule	Lee	5/8/2005		Navy	
Crazymule	Thomas				Legion
Crazymule	Xavier				Museum
Cummins	Richard Walker	5/12/1942	5/31/1946	Army	
Curley	Billford			Army	Museum
Curley	Joe, Jr			Army	Museum
Curley	Joe, Sr			Army	Museum
Curley	Login			Army	Museum
Dahle	Edwin			Navy	Legion
Divesbackwards	Sam		2/15/1945		Legion
Divesbackwards	Strine	-/7/1943	2/22/1946	Army	Legion
Eaglefeathers	Anthony			Army	
Eaglefeathers	Milton				Legion
Eaglefeathers	Oliver, Glenn		6/10/1960	Army	
Eaglefeathers	Toni			Army	

Last Name	First Name	Date Enlisted	Date Discharged	Branch	Source
Eastman	Dalmer K				
Eastman	Robert				Legion
Elkshoulder	Andrew			Marine	
Elkshoulder	Leonard	1/14/1966	1/14/1969	Army	
Elkshoulder	Mark				
Elliott	Ervin		4/14/1977	Army	Legion
Elliott	Myron L				Legion
Ewing	Pierre				
Farr	Frank	4/24/1944	12/5/1944	Army	Legion
Fightingbear	Herbert	10/17/1942	11/9/1945	Army	Legion
Firecrow	Joseph	1945	1947		Legion
Fisher	Bernadine	11/1/1945	1947	Army	Legion
Fisher	Daniel Sr			Army	
Fisher	Emery Sidney		1982	Army	
Fisher	Floyd	1955	1958	Navy	Legion
Fisher	James	10/31/1944	11/8/1945	Navy	Legion
Fisher	Jason Jerry	1961	1964	Army	
Fisher	Phillips Brother				Museum
Fisher	Russell				Legion
Fishing Hawk	Curtis	1977	1990	Army Navy Seals	Family
Flatness	Kellie				
Flatness	Lonnie			Marine	Museum
Flatness	Ollie			Army	Museum
Flores	Angeline				
Flores	Anthony			Army	
Flying	John Paul			Army	
Flying	Larry	1/15/1968	7/10/1970	Marine	
Flying	Parker				Legion
Foot	James				
Foote	Adrian			Army	
Foote	Edward Jr			Marine	
Foote	Joseph				
Foote	Richard			Army	
Fox	Deanna			Marine	
Fox	Joe Sr				Legion
Gardipe	George R	8/13/1942	12/25/1945		
Glenmore	Floyd	1963	1967	Army	Museum
Glenmore	Ronnie	1964	1965	Army	Museum
Gray	Eddie	1997	2000	Marine	
Gray	Joe, Jr			Navy	
Gray	Teddy	3/20/1941	3/16/1946	Army	Legion
Green	Tambouzi			Army	
Grinsell	Edward, Jr			Army	Museum
Grinsell	Edward Sr			Air Force	Museum
Grinsell	Floyd			Army	Museum
Grinsell	John J			Army	Museum
Grinsell	William J			Army	Museum
Hairy Hand				Scout	
Hardground	Francis				
Hardground	Thomas M	11/3/1950	3/21/1956	Army	Legion
Hardrobe	Colonel	10/27/1876	4/20/1891		
Harris	Chester			Air Force	Legion
Harris	Clinton	1965	1967	Army	
Harris	Francis			Air Force	Legion
Harris	George	1/20/1942	10/5/1945	Marine	Legion
Harris	Gilbert				Museum

Last Name	First Name	Date Enlisted	Date Discharged	Branch	Source
Harris	Lafavette Lafe			Navy	
Hart	Eugene			Army	Museum
Hart	Robert			Army	Museum
Haselbun	Homer				
Hawk Inee				Scout	
Headswirt	Wayne	10/6/1967	10/7/1970	Army	
Heart	Hubert			Navy	
Hill	Shandon			Army	
Hisbadhorse	Ernest	12/15/1942	12/15/1944	Army	Legion
Hiwalker	Hank				Museum
Hiwalker	George III	4/5/1977		Army	
Hiwalker	Weaver	1966	1968	Marine	
High Walking	Frank			Army	
High Walking	Micah Rae			Army	
Hollowbreast	William	7/11/1917	6/20/1919	Army	
Horn	Harold				
Horn	Harold, Jr			Army	Museum
Horn	Kenneth M	1973	1975	Army	Museum
Horn	Mike	1972	1976	Army Ranger	Museum
Horn	Miles			Army	Museum
Horn	Steven			Army	Museum
Horn	Bruce			Marine	Museum
Horn	Denver			Marine	Museum
Hurff	Mollie	2003	2006	Army	
Iron Hand	Rufus	1951	1955	Air Force	Legion
Issues	John	5/3/1890	4/2/1891	Troop A	
Issues	Ira	1949	1951	Army	
Issues	Irene	1/25/1944	3/9/1946	WAC	Legion
Johnson	Wolfe				
Jones	Hugh, O				
Kellum	Bruce			Army	
Kellum	George				
Kills On Top	Frank				
Kills On Top	Harold	6/22/51		Air Force	
Kills On Top	Peter				
Kills On Top	Rufus			Army	
Kills On Top	Troy	1984	1990	Army / N Guard	
Killsnight	Avon				Legion
Killsnight	Eli				Legion
Killsnight	Ferdinand				
Killsnight	Marcian			Army	
Killsnight	Martin			Army	Museum
Killsontop	Frank				Legion
Killsontop	Harold				Legion
Killsontop	Paul				Legion
King	Eva Littlewolf				Legion
King	James D Sr	8/22/1941	10/28/1945	Air Force	Legion
King	Raymond			Marine	Museum
King	Rudolph Sr	7/8/1943	12/26/1945	Army	Museum
King	Rudolph, Jr	5/18/1970	3/16/1973	Army	
Knowshisgun	Hector			Air Force	Legion
La Rance	Christopher				Legion
La Rance	Henry				
Laforge	Benjamin				
Lafountan	Anthony	1980	1981	Army	
Lafountan	Anthony, Jr			Army	

Last Name	First Name	Date Enlisted	Date Discharged	Branch	Source
Lafountain	Tammy			Army	
Lahn	Burt			Coast Guard	
Lahn	Catherine			Air Force	
Lame Woman	Virgil			Army	Museum
Larance	Albert				Legion
Larance	Christopher				Legion
Larance	Maynard				
Last Bull	Fred				Museum
Limberhand	Elmer Sr	4/24/1944	11/11/1945	Army	Legion
Limberhand	Elmer, Jr	1949	1953	Army	Museum
Limberhand	Maurice, Sr			Army	Museum
Limpy	Francis				Legion
Limpy	Fred			Army	
Limpy	Fred, Jr			Army	
Limpy	Homer	1962	1963	Army	
Limpy	Lisa			Army	Museum
Little Bear	Cleveland Lance	1966	1969	Army	Museum
Little Bear	Pete				Legion
Little Bear	Richard			Army	Museum
Little Bird	Glenda			Marine	Museum
Little Bird	Harry				Legion
Little Bird	James	1942	1946	Army	Museum
Little Bird	Joe			WWII	Museum
Little Bird	Joey			Marine	Museum
Little Bird	Lloyd			Marine	Museum
Little Coyote	Barry				
Little Coyote	Eugene			Air Force	Legion
Little Coyote	Monte	2002	2003	Army	Museum
Little Coyote	Perry				
Little Mouth	Mike				
Little Mouth	Preston				Legion
Littlesun	Alfred	2/??/42	5/22/1945	Army	Museum
Littlesun	Horace	1942	1945	Army	Legion
Littlebear	Paul				
Littlebird	Harry				
Littlebird	James	6/15/1942	4/6/1946	Army	
Little Coyote	Eugene			Air Force	Legion
Little Coyote	Monte Jr	2002	2003	Army	
Littlehead	Charles			8th Cavalry	
Littlehead	George				Legion
Littlesun	Horace				Legion
Littlewhirlwind	Anthony			Navy	
Littlewhirlwind	Benidice			Army	Museum
Littlewhirlwind	Blaine			Army Airborne	Museum
Littlewhirlwind	Cletis Lockwood			Navy	
Littlewhirlwind	Howard			Legion	
Littlewhirlwind	Joseph				Legion
Littlewhiteman	David, Jr	1974	1980	Navy	
Littlewhiteman	David, Sr	1951	1954	Air Force	Museum
Littlewhiteman	Tom			Army	
Littlewhiteman	Wayne F	1946	12/31/1946	Marine	Legion
Littlewolf	George				Legion
Littlewolf	Lanard				
Locker	Walter Rusty			Vietnam	Museum
Loneelk	George	1950		Army	Museum
Loneelk	Manuel			Navy	

Last Name	First Name	Date Enlisted	Date Discharged	Branch	Source
Loneelk	Wilson				Legion
Lonebear	Bob		10/5/1955		Museum
Lonebear	Robert	11/5/1943	12/4/1945	Air Force	
Long Sioux	Clifford			Army	Museum
Longjaw	John				Legion
Longjaw	Joseph			Marine	
Longjaw Marshall	Arthur	11/20/1950	11/3/1953	Army	Legion
Looks Behind	Leonard			Army	Museum
Mac Fadden	Fred	7/24/2008	4/6/2019	Air Force	
Magpie	James			Army	
Magpie	Malina			Navy	
McMakin	James	11/11/1941	7/31/1945	Army	
Medicine Bull	Bert				Legion
Medicine Bull	Fred Jr			Army	Museum
Medicine Elk	Bruce			Army	Museum
Medicine Elk	Colin			Army	
Medicine Elk	James	1963			Museum
Medicine Elk	Peter	10/12/1944	11/12/1946	Army	Legion
Medicine Elk	Thomas		2/13/1938	Air Force	Legion
Medicine Elk	Wayne			Army	Legion
Medicine Top	John			Army	Museum
Mexican Cheyenne		11/27/1890	6/11/1892	8th Cavalry	
Miles, Seminole	Nelson			8th Cavalry	
Moore	Charlotte Louise			2003	Marine
Morgan	Claude				
Morrison	Cedrick			Marine	
Mullin	James I	11/25/1942	1/18/1946	Army	
Mullin	James N				
Ness	Clayton			Marine	
Old Bull	James				Legion
Old Mouse	Roger	6/9/1961	8/11/1965	Air Force	
One Bear	Jim			Army	Museum
One Bear	Robert			Air Force	Legion
One Bear	Wayne	1950	1953	Army	Legion
Parker	Clyde			Army	
Parker	Edwin				Legion
Parker	Gabriel				Legion
Parker	Lyle				Legion
Parker	Morris				Legion
Parker	Shirley				Legion
Parker	Winfred				Legion
Parker Peters	George Stephen			Marine	
Peck	Francis	2/15/1954	5/14/1954	Army	
Phipps	Jesse			Army	
Pittman	Robert	11/28/1950	1953	Marine	Museum
Pittman	Roy H		2/21/1920	Navy	
Prairie Bear	Aloysius				Legion
Pretty Boy	Mario, Jr			Army	
Red Bird	Lyle				Legion
Red Bird	Samuel				Legion
Red Cherries	Frank				Legion
Red Cherries	Merlyn Lee			Marine	Museum
Red Cherries	Adolph	1951		Army	Legion
Red Cherries	Carol	2/23/1955	8/4/1960	Air Force	
Red Fox	Ervin				Legion
Red Fox	Ralph				Legion

Last Name	First Name	Date Enlisted	Date Discharged	Branch	Source
Redcloud, Bigfoot	Carl Pete	2/6/1943		Army	
Redrobe	Jasper				Legion
Redwoman	Dominic				
Ridgebear	Jerry	1950		Army	Museum
Ridgebear	One	12/7/1977	3/11/1978		
Ridgewalker				Scout	
Riding In	Cecil	5/21/1941	10/15/1945	Marine	
Risingsun	Collins				Legion
Risingsun	Harry	2/2/1943	4/1/1946	Army	Legion
Risingsun	Peter			Air Force	Museum
Risingsun	Phillip	1890	1891	Scout	
Risingsun	Teddy	1951		Army	Legion
Robinson	Bee				
Robinson	Buell D	1/4/1951	12/29/1952	Army	Legion
Robinson	Cornelius	5/24/1944	10/18/1944	Army	Legion
Robinson	Lynwood			Army	
Rockroads	Tom Jr			Army	Museum
Roundstone	Wayne			Army	Museum
Roundstone	Wendell			Army	Museum
Rowland	Allen				Legion
Rowland	Donald				Legion
Rowland	Eugene			Prison, Korea	Museum
Rowland	Frank				Legion
Rowland	Rex				Legion
Rowland	Richard Leroy			Army	
Rowland	Willis T			Troop L 8th	
Runsabove	Leroy			Army	Museum
Runsabove	Lloyd L	5/29/1944	1/30/1945	Navy	
Russell	Clifford			Army	Legion
Russell	Harry				Legion
Russell	Hubert				Legion
Russell	John Jr	10/5/1966	10/4/1972	Army	
Russell	Winfield				Museum
Ryan	Van Sr			Army	Museum
Sampson	Aaron Boyd		9/27/1984	Marine	
Sandcrane	Edward	1950		Army	Museum
Sandcrane	James				
Sandcrane	Joe	1950		Army	Museum
Sandcrane	Michael	5/2/1960	5/14/1964	Army	
Sandcrane	Peter				Legion
Sandcrane	Henry	4/23/1942	9/10/1945		Legion
Schwartz	Joe H		6/11/1946	Army	
Selage	James			Army	Museum
Selage	May				Museum
Selage	Nicholas M				
Seminole	Burton			Army	Museum
Seminole	Emmanuel, Jr	1990	1994	Army	Family
Seminole	Eugene			Marine	Museum
Seminole	Frederick Dale, Jr				Navy L
Seminole	John	1950		Army	Museum
Seminole	Ronald				Museum
Seminole	Miles				
Seminole	Stephen			Marine	
Shanta	Miranda			Army	
Shavehead	Francis	1950		Army	Museum
Sherman	Oliver C				Legion

Last Name	First Name	Date Enlisted	Date Discharged	Branch	Source
Shoulderblade	Berndine	12/8/1970	12/7/1976	Army	
Shoulderblade	Francis	5/11/1942	8/13/1944	Army	Legion
Shoulderblade	James			WWII	Museum
Shoulderblade	Windelyn Valdo	1/8/1970	2/22/1972	Army	Legion
Simpson	Earl Thomas			Army	
Siouxcalf	Laforce			Marine	
Sloan	Roger				
Small	Clinton				Legion
Small	Edward				Legion
Small	George	2/5/1943	7/26/1946	Army	
Small	Horace			Army	Museum
Small	Ivan				Legion
Small	John				Legion
Small	Kim			Navy	
Small	Max				Legion
Small	Melvin				Legion
Small	Ralph				Legion
Small	Thomas			WWII	Museum
Small	Worth R				Legion
Smith	George J	2/5/1943	7/26/1946	Army	
Soldier	Manford				
Solis	Carl	1967	1968	Vietnam	Museum
Solis	Joseph			Army	
Spang	Dylan			Army	
Spang	Donald				Legion
Spang	Edward				Museum
Spang	Jake			Army Reserve	
Spang	Lyman				Legion
Spang	Marvin			Army	
Spang	Norman			Navy	Museum
Spang	Pete				Museum
Spang	Wilber			Army	Museum
Spang	Wilber Sr	1967	1969	Army	Museum
Spear	James Bites Jr				
Speelman	Benjamin			Army	
Speelman	Ervin				
Speelman	Gilbert			Navy	
Speelman	Irvin Lee			Army	Legion
Speelman	Jeffery			Air Force	
Speelman	Leslie		2002	Marine	
Speelman	Orville			Air Force	Legion
Speelman	William				Legion
Spotted Eagle	Douglas	1966	1968	Army	
Spotted Elk	Abraham			Marine	Museum
Spotted Elk	Charles				
Spottedwolf	James	10/16/1950	10/15/1953	Army	Legion
Spottedwolf	Jennie Lou			Navy	
Spottedwolf	John				Legion
Squint Eyes	John	1920		Scout	Museum
Standing Elk	Benno	8/4/1949	12/20/1950		Legion
Standing Elk	Edwin	4/21/1969	1970	Marine	
Standing Elk	Eugene				
Standing Elk	George	4/6/1951	3/6/1955	Air Force	Legion
Standing Elk	Melvin			Army	
Standing Elk	Wayne				Legion
Standsintimber	John Jr			Navy	Museum

Last Name	First Name	Date Enlisted	Date Discharged	Branch	Source
Stange Owl	Alfred			Navy	Museum
Strange Owl	Gabriel			Army	
Strange Owl	Gordon			Army	Museum
Sweetmedicine	Willie				Legion
Stumphorn	Frank	9/7/1879	4/30/1895	Scout, 5th Infantry	
Tall Bull	Charles			Army	Museum
Tall Bull	Floyd			Army	Museum
Tall Bull	Neil			Marine	Museum
Tall Bull	Nelson, Jr			Army	Museum
Tall Bull	Nelson, Sr			Army	Museum
Tall Bull	Wayne Allen			Marine	Museum
Tallbull	Albert	1965			Museum
Tallbull	Charles				
Tallbull	Edmond		1966	Army	Museum
Tallbull	Joe Jr			Army	Museum
Tallbull	Lloyd		2006	Army	
Tallbull	Lynwood	1965		Army	Museum
Tallbull	Russell	1950		Army	Museum
Tallbull	Thomas Craig		2005		
Tallbull	Vern				Museum
Tallbull	William	8/30/1942	11/20/1945	Army	Museum
Tallwhiteman	Clarence		1/2/1951	Killed, Korea	Legion
Tallwhiteman	Jasper				Legion
Tallwhiteman	Raymond			Navy	Legion
Tallwhiteman	Russell			Army	Museum
Teeth	Austin	1969		Army	Museum
Teeth	Lincoln	1/9/1976	3/25/1977	Marine	
Teeth El-Vase	Charles			Indian Wars	
Threefingers	Antone			Army	
Threefingers	Jack Johnson		8/22/1985	Army	
Threefingers	Jessica			Army	
Threefingers	Joseph			Army	Museum
Threefingers	Joseph III			Army	Museum
Threefingers	Judas	1998	2006	Marine	
Threefingers	Tony			Army	Museum
Thunderbird	Richard			Cavalry	
Timber	John Gilbert			Navy	
Trout	Neil	1965	1971	Marine	
Turtle	Jacqueline	1983	1989	Marine	
Trusty	Theresa				Legion
Twobulls	Joseph				Legion
Twomoons	Austin				Legion
Two Moons	Billy			Army	
Two Moons	Matthew				Legion
Two Two	Raymond Sr			Army	Museum
Two Two	Stephen Jr				Legion
Two Two	Vincent			Army	Museum
Underwood	Harold	1944	1946	WWII	Museum
Walker	Alonzo	8/2/1968	9/3/1971	Army	
Walker	Jerry			Army	
Walker	Sam	6/1/2005	6/1/2005	Army	
Walksalong	Joe				
Walksalong	Laroche			Army	
Walkslast	Gilbert			Army	Legion
Walkslast	James	1968	1970	Army	Museum
Walkslast	Joe			Army	Museum

Last Name	First Name	Date Enlisted	Date Discharged	Branch	Source
Walksnice	Leroy				Legion
Wallowing Hill	Shandon	2002	2003	Army	
Walters	Bristle Coolidge	1950		Army	Museum
Walters	Ford Buford			Scout	
Walters	George			Scout	Museum
Wandering Medicine	Lomar			Marine	Museum
Wandering Medicine	Mark				Museum
Waters	Joe Jr	1974	1976	Army	Museum
Waters	Joseph Sr	1951	1954	Army	
Weaselbear	Elroy Jay	1995	1999	Marine	Museum
Weaselbear	Robert				Legion
White	Stamper				Museum
White	Wallis	1950		Army	Museum
White	Willis				Legion
White Shield	Steven	1974	1978	Marine	
White Crane	Jasper			Army	Museum
Whitedirt	Charles	1965			Museum
Whitedirt	Doreen			Army	Museum
Whitedirt	Patrick	1950		Army	Museum
Whitehawk	Andrew				Legion
Whiteman	Clarence		10/16/1951	Killed, Korea	Museum
Whiteman	Frank Paul			Air Force	
Whiteman	Leroy				Legion
Whiteman	Milton Buster				Legion
Whiteman	Richard				
Whiteman	Willis				Legion
Whitewolf	Calvin			Army	Museum
Whitewolf	Daniel	9/19/1961	10/15/1964	Marine	
Whitewolf	Isadore			Navy	
Whitewolf	Leo				Legion
Whitewolf	Joe	2/9/1944	11/2/1945	Army	Legion
Whitewolf	Joe	1965			Museum
Whitewoman	Vernell			Navy	
Wild Hog	Adam				Legion
Wild Hog	John	5/3/05		Army	
Wild Hog	John	1/7/1882	1/6/1883	Scout/Ft Reno	
Wild Hog	John Bird	9/18/1890	5/15/1891	Hunter 8th	
Wilson	Arthur				Legion
Wilson	Curley	1950	1953	Army	Museum
Wilson	Michael			Marine	
Wilson	George C				Legion
Wilson	Peter			Marine	
Wilson	James				Legion
Wilson Curly	William Alfred	12/29/1950	12/8/1953	Army	Legion
Wolfblack	Henry				Legion
Wolfblack	Oran C				Legion
Wolf Name	William	5/3/1890	4/30/1891	Troop A	
Wolfchief	Harshey	11/27/1890	1/20/1891		
Wolfchief	Lyman Jr			Army	
Wolfchief	Niles			Army	
Wolfchief	Norman	3/4/1947	8/30/1948	Army	Legion
Wolfchum	Francis				
Wolfchum	John F				Legion
Wolfname	Ciciley			Army Airborne	
Wolfname	Forrest Daniel				
Wolfroads	Paul				Legion

Last Name	First Name	Date Enlisted	Date Discharged	Branch	Source
Wolfvoice	Dewey				Legion
Wooden Legs	John Joseph	9/27/1967	5/25/1970	Army	
Wooden Legs	Matthew				Legion
Woodenthigh	Teddy				Legion
Woundeye	Melvin	8/1/1941	10/12/1945	Army	Legion
White	Willis				Legion
Yellowhair	Patrick				Legion
Yelloweyes	David				Legion
Yellowfox	Charles				Museum
Yellowrobe	Lloyd				
Yellowrobe	Moses	5/26/1947	2/10/1948	Air Force	Legion
Yellowrobe	Uydell	1995	1999	Marine	Museum
Yellowrobe	Vydel Ross	Sept 1995	Sept 1999	Marine	Museum
Yellowrobe	Waldo				Legion
Yellowrobe	William	1890	3/??/1905	Casey's Soldier	
Young Bear	Arthur				Legion
Youngbear	Benjamin George		12/16/1966	9/1/1969	Army
Youngbear	Leonard			Marine	Museum

Northern Cheyenne Active Duty and Unknown Status List
As of December 2007

This list was compiled primarily by Janet Mullin. The people who worked on this list tried to include everyone, but there are undoubtedly omissions, especially in the list from the 1880s. If someone has been omitted, contact Janet Mullin at the Jessie Mullin Picture Museum in Lame Deer (406) 477-6460

Last Name	First Name	Branch of Service	Status
Bahr	Michael Ray	Marine	Active
Beckman	Jason	Army	Active
Blackwolf	Hubert, Jr	Airborne	Active
Bullcoming	Wilson	Army	Unknown
Fisher	Eugene, Jr	Air Force	Unknown
Fisher	Lance R	Marine	Active
Kellum	George Anthony	Army	Active
Lei	John, Jr	Army	Active
Lei	Robby	Army	Active
Mann	Fred	Army	Reserves
Pretty Boy	John	Army	Active
Rising Sun - Glenn	Josie	Army	Active
Roundstone	Harlan	Marine	Unknown
Roundstone	Jewel	Army	Unknown
Shoulderblade	Julius	Army	Unknown
Snow	Kristen	Air Force	Active
Two Two	Tyson	Marine	Active
Two Two	Uriah	Army	Active
Zimmer	Tristin	Navy	Unknown

APPENDIX B

Tribal Presidents

Rufus Wallowing
December 1935-September 1936

Joseph White Bear
September 1936-June 1938

Eugene Fisher
September 1938-May 1940

William Red Cherries
June 1940-January 1943

John Stands in Timber
March 1943-July 1943

William Red Cherries
July 1943- September 1944

Eugene Fisher, Sr
September 1944-July 1947

John Russell
July 1947-September 1948

Rufus Wallowing
September 1948-September 1952

Eugene Fisher, Sr
September 1952-March 1955

John Wooden Legs
March 1955 – September 1968

Allan Rowland
September 1968 – September 1984

Windy Shoulder Blade
September 1984 – December 1985

Mark Elk Shoulder
December 1985 – January 30, 1986
August 18, 1986 – August 30, 1986

John Buffalo Horn
January 1986 – August 1986

Charles Yellow Fox
August 1986 – September 1986

Robert Bailey
September 1986 – October 1986
October 1986 – September 1988

Edwin Dahle
September 1988 – December 1989

John Wooden Legs, Jr
December 1989 – January 1990

Edwin Dahle
January 1990 – November 1992

Llevando Fisher
September 1992 – December 1996

William Walks Along
December 1996 – January 1998

Norma Gourneau
January 1998 – March 1998

Joe Walks Along, Sr
March 1998 – November 2000

Geri Small
November 2000 – 2004

Eugene Little Coyote
November 2004 – February 2008

Geri Small
February 2008 – Present

This list was compiled by the Northern Cheyenne TeCH Project It was retrieved by Patti Means on June 13, 2007, from the website http /btc montana edu/tech/Northern_Cheyenne/NC_Presidents htm

Index

Note: *Italicized* page numbers indicate
illustrations and the accompanying captions

orphans, in creation stories 20
Owens, Nancy, 136
ownership, individual vs. tribal 58, 147

P-20 movement, 111
paint, as adornment in creation stories, 18–19
Parental Involvement Program in Education
    project, 105
Pawnees, in creation stories 20
Peabody Coal Company, 135, 139
peace pipes, 71–72, 72
pemmican, 65, 66
Pennsylvania State University, 128
people pollution, 138
Petter, Rodolphe, 36, 47
Petter Alphabet, 36
Pine Ridge Agency, 27 (map), 30, 49
pipes and pipe smoking, 71–72, 72
Platero, Dillon, 42
pollution, 138, 148
    see also air quality
poverty, 101, 121–122, 135, 137, 142, 149
Powell, Peter J., 85
Pratt, Richard Henry 89–90
Prevention of Significant Deterioration regula-
    tions, 138–139
Pringle, Robert M., 57, 61n12
prisoners held at Fort Marion, 90–91
prisoners of war, World War II, 73
Prunus virginiana (chokecherry), 65–66
public high schools, 102
Public Law 874, 107
Punished Woman's Fork, 27 (map)

Rabbit Town, 48
Race Track, 18
racism, 42–43, 115, 133–135
rage, suppressed, 41
ranching vs. farming, 56–59
rations 25, 50, 56
reburials, 23–25 80–84, 146
Red Cloud Agency 28
Red Lodge mine, 131
Red Tassel in creation stories, 20
Ree Ceremony 53
Ree Tribe (Arikara Tribe), 51
relocation projects, effects of, 41, 68–70
Reno, Janet, 111
repatriation of American Indian remains,
    23–25, 84, 146
reservations
    agriculture and economy of, 60

reservations (continued)
    importance of, to American Indian people,
        146–147
    poverty on, 101, 121–122, 135, 142, 149
    resources, control of 142
    sale of surplus land, 58, 141
    surplus land of, 141
    see also individual reservation names
Rising Bull, 90
Risingsun, Ted
    and battle to protect land 146
    and Colstrip project, 140
    on Dull Knife, 115
    and Indian-controlled school board, 106
    memory of Indian New Deal programs, 59
    as tribal spokesman to Consol, 136–137
Robinson, Tommy B., 117
Rocky Mountain College, 123
Roman Nose, 87, 90, 92
Rosa arkansara (Rose Bush) 64
Rosebud County, 138
Rosebud/Ree District 51
rose hips 64
Rosenfelt, Daniel M., 105
Rowland, Allen, 136, 142, 173
Rowland, Franklin, 76
Rural Systemic Initiative (RSI), 125, 126
Russell, John, 132, 173
Rustling Corn Leaf, 21
Ryan, John D., 132

Sacred Arrow Keeper, 88
Sacred Arrows, 85, 87, 88
Sacred Arrow Worship ceremony 142
sacred ceremonies, 45, 53, 142
Sacred Hat, 23, 88
Sacred Mountain, 18
Sacred Woman, 88
Salish Tribe, 141, 147
Sand Creek Battle, 27 (map), 83
Sanders, Jeffrey 105
Sand Hills of Nebraska, 70
Sandoz, Mari, 132–133, 150
Sarvisberry (Amelanchier alnifolia) 64–65
Scabby People Place, 49
scalp shirts 137
schools see education, specific schools
Seminole, Louie, 54
sexism, 68
Shave Head, 90
Shepherdia canadensis (Buffalo Berry), 65
Shoulderblade, Pius, 59–60

Ingram Content Group UK Ltd.
Milton Keynes UK
UKHW022015130323
418525UK00005B/92